# South Korea

# South Korea

Joan  Beard

Little Hills Press

First Edition, **July 1997**
© Joan Beard, 1997


General Map of Korea by MAPgraphics
All other maps © Korea National Tourism Corporation
© Photographs, Korea National Tourism Corporation

Cover by NB Design

Published by
**Little Hills Press Pty Ltd**
Regent House, 37-43 Alexander Street,
Crows Nest, NSW, 2065
Australia
email Address: littlehills@peg.apc.org
Home Page: http://www.peg.apc.org/~littlehills

ISBN 1 86315 088 9

## DISCLAIMER

Whilst all care has been taken by the author to ensure that the information is up to date and accurate, the publisher does not take responsibility for the information published herein. As things get better or worse, places close and others open, some elements in the book may be inaccurate when you get there. Please write and tell us about it so we can update in subsequent editions.


LITTLE HILLS and  are registered trademarks of Little Hills Press Pty Ltd.


## ACKNOWLEDGEMENTS

The Publishers wish to thank the Korea National Tourism Corporation for providing the photographs and maps for this publication. A special thank you to Jennifer Doherty of the Korea National Tourism Organization, Sydney for her assistance and advice.

# Contents

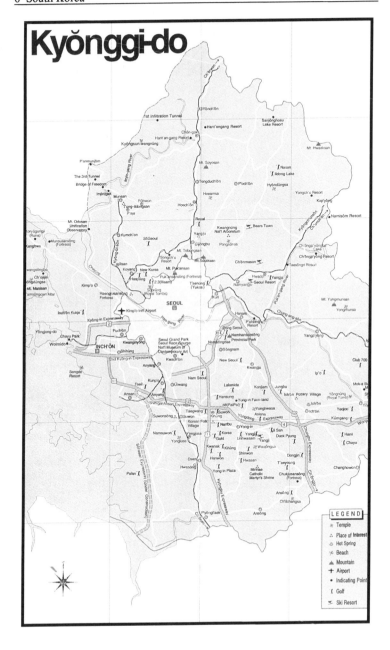

# Introduction

Korea is a peninsula in eastern Asia bordered by China in the north. It was divided into two countries in 1948.

South Korea, Taehan-Minguk (Republic of Korea), has an area of about 98,447 sq km, and is estimated to be about 480 km long by 298 km wide. Its highest peak, Halla-San Mountain, is 1950m above sea level.

The capital is Seoul, and the chief port is Pusan. There are 3300 islands to the south and south-west of the peninsula.

Administratively the Republic of South Korea consists of nine provinces which are further divided into 68 cities (*shi*) and 136 counties (*gun*), five metropolitan cities and the capital.

Seoul City has a population of 10.6 million making it one of the largest cities in Asia. The five metropolitan cities are: Pusan (3.8 million), Taegu (2.2 million), Inch'on (1.8 million), Kwangju (1.1 million), and Taejon (1.1 million).

## History

Long before the birth of Christ, the first Korean state was developed along the Taedong River. It was called Choson, meaning "Land of the Morning Calm". In 108BC China conquered the northern part of the peninsula and set up four territories. The Korean tribes had won back three of these tracts of land by 75BC, but the fourth, Lelang, remained under Chinese control.

During the 2nd century AD several Korean tribes united and formed the state of Koguryo in the north-eastern part of the peninsula. Two other states, Paekche and Silla, were established in the south during the 3rd century AD. They were known by historians as *The Three Kingdoms*. Buddhism, which the Koreans had learned from the Chinese, became the chief religion.

In 313 Koguryo conquered Lelang, driving the Chinese forces

out of the north. Silla conquered both Paekche and Koguryo in the 600s and took control of the entire peninsula. Confucianism was introduced into Silla and became a strong influence on thought and behaviour.

During the 800s Silla started to break apart but was reunited in 932 by General Wang Kon. He renamed the country Koryo, and the name Korea came from this word. The government of Koryo worked hard to encourage education. It stimulated printing so that more books would be available. The Koreans developed the first movable metal printing type in 1234.

Since the early 1200s, Mongol tribes from the north had been attacking Koryo, and in 1259 they conquered it. The Koreans freed themselves in 1368, and the two groups fought for control until 1388 when General Yi Songgye was victorious. He became king in 1392 and renamed the country Choson. This name remained until the 1940s.

Japanese forces invaded Korea in the 1590s but were driven out by the Manchu armies who conquered Korea. The Manchus received tribute payments from the Koreans until the late 1800s but the Yi family continued as kings. At the beginning of the 1600s, the Korean rulers closed the country to all foreigners for two-hundred years. The people had little contact with any country except China.

Catholic missionaries from Europe entered Korea during the 1830s, but the authorities persecuted them, and killed thousands of inhabitants who had become Catholics.

In 1876 the Japanese forced the Koreans to open their ports to trade. After Japan won the Chinese-Japanese War of 1894-95, their influence on Korea became stronger than that of China, and in 1910 they took complete control. They set up many industries and put them under Japanese management. They also took much of the Korean land and sold it to Japanese settlers. Japan ruled Korea until 1945 when US troops occupied the southern half and Russian forces took control of the northern section. For two years, the United States and Russia, with the two Korean States, tried to reunite the country as one. This failed and the problem was turned over to the United Nations in 1947.

### Since 1948

The UN wanted to supervise elections to choose one government for Korea but the Russians refused to allow the UN representatives into the North. In 1948 the UN supervised elections in the South and the National Assembly drew up a constitution. They elected Syngman Rhee as President of the Republic of Korea in August 1948. The communists in the north announced the formation of the Democratic People's Republic in September. Both parties claimed to represent the whole of Korea. In December 1948, the USSR announced that it had withdrawn all its troops from North Korea, and the last American troops left South Korea in mid-1949. In June 1950 North Korean troops attacked the South and the Korean war began. Neither side won complete victory.

In 1983 a Soviet Union military plane shot down a South Korean passenger aircraft which had flown into their airspace, killing all 269 people on board. Later that year, a bomb blast killed 17 South Koreans, including four cabinet ministers, on an official visit to Rangoon, Myanmar. The South Koreans accused the Northern agents of the bombings. In recent times, the USA has been worried that North Korea has developed a nuclear bomb with the intention of reclaiming the South.

### South Korea

After the division, South Korea was left with little industry and few electric power plants. Also, the fighting had ruined the crops. During the 1950s the National Assembly became increasingly critical of Rhee for failing to solve the economic problems. By the end of the decade Rhee had lost more support and began to use undemocratic methods to keep control of the government. Although he was re-elected in 1952, 1956 and March 1960, his party had to "fix" the election of the Vice Presidential candidate to ensure victory. There were widespread demonstrations against the government, led by students, and Rhee resigned in April. In July 1960 elections were again held. The economic difficulties continued and rival groups fought for political power.

In May 1961 a group of military officers led by General Park Chung Hee overthrew the government. In 1963 Park called elections to restore democratic rule. He won the election and became President and his Democratic Republican party won the majority of seats. South Korea's economy developed rapidly under Park. He concentrated on foreign trade and industry. In 1972 voters approved various constitutional amendments after the government had declared martial law. Park frequently used his power to hold down opposition to his government. Freedom of speech and the press were limited and numerous opponents of Park were gaoled. Many denounced him as a dictator. President Park was assassinated by Kim Jae Kyu, leader of the South Korean CIA (Agency of National Security Planning) in October 1979. Prime Minister Choi Kyu Han became acting head of state, and in December was elected president. Choi ended some of the restrictions on freedom that had existed under Park. The government delayed a promise to allow the election of the President to be made by the people. There were many demonstrations.

In May 1980 South Korea's military leaders declared martial law and re-established restrictions on freedom of expression. Choi remained president but the military, led by Lieutenant General Chun Doo Hwan, dominated the government. Violent demonstrations took place in the city of Kwangju and hundreds of demonstrators were killed. In August 1980 Choi resigned, Chun was elected by the Electoral College, and a constitutional amendment provided that the president could not be re-elected. Chun ended martial law. He scheduled elections and ran for president unopposed. The students demonstrated once more. In 1987 Chun pledged to allow direct election of the president by the people. An election was held in December, and Roh Tae Woo of the Democratic Justice Party was elected president. In 1990 his party merged with the Reunification Democratic Party and the New Democratic Republican Party to form the Democratic Liberal Party.

## Climate

Korea has a temperate climate. It is situated in the transitional zone between continental and subtropical maritime climates.

There are four distinct seasons:

**Spring**. Late March through May, with temperatures beginning to rise in March. Cherry blossoms bloom in early April and forsythia, azaleas, magnolias and lilacs in late April.

**Summer**. June to early September is hot and humid.

Temperatures can rise to 35C. Half the annual rainfall occurs during the monsoon months of late June and July. Mid-July to mid-August is the hottest period and also the height of the Korean vacation season.

**Autumn.** September through November. Brings warm days, cool nights, clear blue sky and spectacular autumn foliage. Many festivals are celebrated in October.

**Winter.** December to mid-March. Intense cold dry spells alternate with periods of milder weather. Temperatures can drop to -20C. Heavy snow falls in the mountains, especially in the area of the ski resorts. There is occasional snow elsewhere.

**Average Temperatures**

| | | | | |
|---|---|---|---|---|
| Seoul | January | -2.6°C | August | 25.5°C |
| Taejon | January | -1.5°C | August | 24.8°C |
| Pusan | January | 3.2°C | August | 23.7°C |
| Cheju | January | 6.5°C | August | 24.8°C |
| Kyongju | January | 1.8°C | August | 23.3°C |

### Clothing

Short sleeved, lightweight cotton clothing is recommended during May-September. A warm coat and sturdy shoes are essential for outdoors in winter.

# Flora and Fauna

The climatic conditions of the Korean peninsula result in a rich and diverse flora. It is best divided into three botanic regions.

The north has alpine flora, conifers such as fir and pines as well as oak, beech, cedar, larch and birch and many types of rhododendrons. In the central region pines and deciduous trees thrive. Trees such as ash, catkins, linden, plane, forsythia and rhododendrons transform the land with their blossoms and foliage.

The south is home to camellias, azaleas and ginkgo trees. It also has many heathers and herbs including ginseng. Korea's indigenous fauna includes the Korean black bear. the mandarin field vole, Tristram's woodpecker, deer, and various kinds of pheasant. There are also many other types of birds, amphibians and reptiles.

Traditionally, the most famous animal is the Korean tiger. Although no longer found on the peninsula, it was once scattered widely throughout the country. The tiger and the bear are the mythical ancestors of the Korean race. Another famous animal is the Chindo dog from the island of the same name. It is a popular watch dog noted for its faithfulness and strength.

# Population

It is estimated that North Korea has a population of around 26,000,000 with 33% living in rural areas. South Korea is estimated to have 44,000,000 residents, with 28% in the rural areas. Cver the last 30 years, there has been a population shift to the cities as South Korea developes its secondary industry.

The annual growth rate is 0.9% and population density is 439.8 people per sq km. The average family size is 3.7 persons, as traditional extended families have decreased and nuclear families have become the norm.

# Education

The first formal school was established in Korea in 372AD, but until the late 1800s, education was available only to those families with high social positions.

Today, education is available to everyone, and school students make up one quarter of the population. Education continues through elementary, middle and high school, to colleges and universities that offer bachelor, master and doctorate degrees in various fields of the arts and sciences.

# Language

The official language is Korean. It has twenty-four letters in its alphabet which is called *han-gul*, and is similar in grammatical structure to Japanese. It is written in a phonetic script called *onmun*. English is spoken in most tourist areas.

### Some useful phrases:

| | |
|---|---|
| Hello - | *Yoboseyo* |
| How do you do? - | *Ch'o-um poep-gessoyo?* |
| Good Morning, afternoon or evening - | *Annyonghaseyo* |

| | |
|---|---|
| I'm glad to meet you - | *Mannaso pan-gawoyo* |
| Good-bye - | *Annyonghi gaseyo* |
| Yes - | *Ye* |
| No - | *Aniyo* |
| Thank you - | *Kamsa hamnida* |
| You are welcome - | *Ch'onmaneyo* |
| Excuse me - | *Shille-hamnida* |
| I am sorry - | *Mian-hamnida* |
| Please help me - | *Towajuseyo* |
| Will you show me the way to Toksugung Palace? - | *Toksugung kanun kirul karuch'o chuseyo?* |
| Where is.....? - | *..... odi issumnikka?* |
| Please go to the ... hotel - | *... ro ka-juseyo* |
| Please stop here - | *Sewo juseyo* |
| Does this bus go to ...? - | *Yi bos-ga ... kamnikka?* |
| Airport - | *Kongbang* |
| Station - | *Yok* |
| Department store - | *Paek'wajom* |
| Duty Free Shop - | *Myonsejom* |
| Bank - | *Unhaeng* |
| Post Office - | *Uch'egok* |
| Police station - | *P'ach'ulso* |
| East Gate Market - | *Tongdaemun sbijang* |
| South Gate Market - | *Namdaemun sbijang* |
| Public Telephone - | *Kongjung-chonhwa* |
| Underground - | *Chihach'ol* |
| Restroom - | *Hwajangsil* |
| How much is it? - | *Olmayejo?* |
| What's this? - | *Igosun muoshimnikka?* |
| I'm just looking around - | *Kugyong chom hagessoyo* |
| That's too expensive - | *Nomu pissayo* |
| Please give it to me - | *Chuseyo* |
| Please bring me the menu - | *Menyu chom chuseyo* |
| The bill, please - | *Kesanso chuseyo* |
| I will have ... - | *... ul mokkessoyo.* |

# Culture

## Architecture

Four factors have shaped Korean architecture: religion; available materials; the natural landscape; and an aesthetic preference for simplicity. Gently sloping roof lines and sturdy undecorated pillars characterise the simplicity, harmony and practical utility of Korean architecture.

Korea has many original wooden and stone structures, some dating back over 1000 years. There are also many skilful reproductions. Traditional architectural designs are incorporated in many modern buildings throughout the country.

## Calligraphy

Calligraphy, the art of brush writing, is a traditional art form in Korea that has exerted a strong influence on social and cultural life. Today it is respected as a revered form of art.

Calligraphy flourished during the Choson Dynasty. The intellectuals and scholars felt that writing was a gift from the gods, and the divine letters and characters were objects of the highest veneration.

Many notable calligraphers created their own styles during the Choson Dynasty. Among the most respected were Prince Anp'yong, Tang Sa'on, Han Sok-bong and King Chong-hui.

## Painting

Tomb murals from the Three Kingdoms Period (1st century BC to 7th century AD) are the earliest examples of Korean painting. Mythological beasts such as dragons and flying horses show a fantastic imagination and creative spirit.

Throughout the Unified Shilla and Koryo Periods, Buddhism prevailed in every field of life, so that a rich collection of icon paintings was produced.

Another painting trend appeared in the late Koryo Dynasty; ink and brush paintings of the four 'noble plants', symbolic of traditional virtues, ie, the plum, orchid, chrysanthemum and bamboo.

The artists of the Choson Dynasty became innovators, with paintings embodying the Korean spirit and perspective. There are humorous animal pictures, scroll paintings of dreamlike, mist-clad mountains, and insightful sketches of everyday life created with brush and ink.

Paintings with themes of folk customs and nature flourished in the latter half of the 18th century. Kim Hong-do and his contemporary Shin Yun-bok were the celebrated masters of this art form.

With the 20th century came Western trends, influencing but not submerging the vibrant tradition of Korean artwork.

### Art Galleries

There are many large and small art galleries in Seoul and its vicinity.' Some of the largest are operated by the public sector. There are many small private galleries in the Apkujong-dong area of southern Seoul and Insa-dong in downtown. Department stores each have their own galleries.

The art galleries frequently host individual and group exhibitions by both Korean and foreign artists, and details of these can be found in the English language dailies.

The major art galleries are located near the drama theatres, concert halls and dance theatres.

Paintings are for sale in private galleries.

*Hoam Art Museum*, 204 Kashil-ri, Yongin-gun, Kyonggi-do, ph (0335) 30 3551.

*Hoam Gallery*, 7, Sunhwa-dong, Chung-gu, Seoul, ph (01) 751 5865.

*Korea Institute of Design and Packaging*, 128-8 Yon-gon-dong, Chongno-gu, Seoul, ph (02) 761 9461.

*National Museum of Contemporary Art*, San 58-1, Makkye-dong, Kwach'on-shi, Kyonggi-do, ph (01) 503 7744.

*Sejong Cultural Centre Art Gallery*, 81-3 Sejongno, Chongno-gu, Seoul, ph (02) 399 1672.

*Seoul Gallery*, 25, T'aep'yongno-1-ga, Chongno-gu, Seoul, ph (02) 735 7711.

### Pottery

Ceramic creativity began with the Neolithic earthenware. The Neolithic hunters and fishers of Korea left only a few examples of comb-pattern pottery.

Most relics from the 5th century AD are burial urns (charnel jars) that show that Buddhism had become widespread. Techniques were developed in producing noteworthy pottery but the skill and beauty of early pottery merely foreshadows the genius of Korean potters in later periods.

One of the most significant achievements in Korean art, the perfection of celadon, was accomplished during the Koryo Dynasty, 936-1392AD. Koreans developed a superbly controlled glaze that was both beautiful and unique because it fully utilised the properties of Korea's rich clay. The highest praise is given to the colour of the glaze, a delicate kingfisher green. Celadon inlaid with a pictorial underglaze decoration is called *sanggam ch'ongja* and it occupies a central position in the category of Koryo celadon. The motifs and decorations found on the celadon are additional reasons for its great popularity among art lovers.

With the beginning of the Choson Dynasty in 1392, there was less emphasis on the ceramic arts. Because the Choson pottery has a strong masculine aesthetic quality, it contrasts sharply with the feminine refinement and elegance of Koryo pottery.

Ich'on Pottery Village in Kyonggi-do, south-east of Seoul, is the site of several potteries and kilns that make reproduction Koryo celadon and Choson white porcelain.

Visitors are free to watch the potters at work and can buy goods from the showrooms. (See *Sightseeing*.)

### Handicrafts

Korea has a long and distinguished history of handicrafts. The government honours the masters by designating them 'human cultural treasurers'. These masters pass on traditions of bow making, drum making, knotting and other traditional skills. Among Korean handicrafts, exquisite wooden chests of the Choson Dynasty are the most famous. Traditional mulberry paper, bamboo baskets, carved wooden items brilliantly inlaid, lacquer-ware, dolls and flower mats also attest to the high quality of Korean traditional handicrafts.

The Human Cultural Assets Handicrafts Gallery, called *Chonsugongbang* in Korean, provides teaching studios for 13 different master craftsmen. At these studios you can watch the master craftsmen at work as well as purchase a wide variety of handicrafts. 944-22 Taech'i-dong, Kangnam-gu, Seoul, ph (02) 565 3482.

Korean Folk Village also provides visitors with a chance to see craftsmen at work. (See *Sightseeing*.)

Many master craftsmen work, and some also reside, at Kyongju Folkcraft Village in Kyongju, ph (0561) 746 7270.

Korea House is also a good place to shop for handicrafts. (See *Sightseeing*.)

## Drama

Traditional Korean dramatic forms include mask dance dramas and chanted narratives. There has been a revival of these dramatic forms and performances are enjoyed by Koreans and foreign visitors alike.

The mask dance is the most popular drama form. Originally, the mask dance was a Buddhist morality play. Until the mid-Choson Dynasty, it was performed at court as an exorcism rite and also as an entertainment. This came to an end when the Neo-Confucianists banished the masked players from the royal court in Seoul.

The mask dance drama continued to thrive in the countryside, however, and it became a comic satire against the privileged class, often depicting the depravity of the aristocratic ruling class, the Buddhist clergy and the triangular relationship between husband, wife and concubine.

## Music and Dance

Koreans have always had a deep love of music and dance. Traditional Korean music is comprised of court and folk music. Court music is slow, solemn and complex. The dances that go with this type of music are stately and highly stylised. Folk music, by contrast, is usually fast and lively with vigorous dancing. Singers go through years of training to cultivate a distinctive sound of their own. Musical performances can be a memorable part of any visit to Korea.

Traditional Korean dance is divided into three main types: court, folk and religious. Among all Korean dances the best known are the fan dance and the drum dance. These are the central performances and are featured in stage shows in various entertainment places, including the Kayagum Theatre Restaurant at the Sheraton Walker Hill Hotel and the Korea House in Seoul.

Of the Korean folk dances, the Farmers Dance is the most popular and exciting. The most graceful of the dances is the Buddhist Nun's Dance in which the performers wear long sleeved coats and high pointed hoods and hold a temple drum. These dances and their musical accompaniments are fine examples of the Korean culture and spirit. Traditional dances are the highlight of national holidays and regional festivals.

Many troupes of dancers and musicians provide a varied program of traditional folk and court music throughout the nation, and internationally as well.

Western music and dance are also performed throughout the country. There are numerous symphony orchestras, chamber music groups, opera companies and talented soloists.

# Religion

South Korea has freedom of religion, which is provided for in the Constitution. It is estimated that 47% of Koreans hold religious beliefs.

Buddhism arrived in the peninsula about 300AD. There are now various different sects comprising some 20% of the population. Confucianism came to Korea around the same time and became the state religion of the Choson Dynasty. Today, though it has strong influence on Korean thought, relationships and family rituals, it is formally practised by just 1% of the population.

Catholicism first aroused only scholarly interest but began to attract true adherents from the end of the 18th century. Its followers now comprise some 5% of the population.

Protestantism was introduced to Korea by missionaries who first arrived in 1885. Today it is the religion of 16% of the people.

Ch'ondogyo is the Korean native religion, founded in 1860 as a reaction to Western influences. It is based on Confucian, Buddhist and Taoist principles, and is practised by a small percentage. Shamanism, Korea's animistic religion, is still followed by a few.

### Religious Services

*Roman Catholic*

Franciscan Chapel (English, Italian, French, German, Spanish), 707 Hannam-dong, Yongsan-gu, Seoul, ph (02) 793 2070.

Myong-dong Cathedral (Korean), 1 Myong-dong 1-ga, Chung-gu, Seoul, ph (02) 774 3890.

*Greek Orthodox*

St Nicholas Orthodox Church (English, Greek), 424-1 Ahyon 1-dong, Map'o-gu, Seoul, ph (02) 362 7005.

*Protestant*

Adventist Church (English), 343-4 Hwigyong 1 dong,

Tongdaemun-gu, Seoul, ph (02) 967 0934.
Anglican Church (English), 3 Chong-dong, Chung-gu, Seoul, ph
(02) 738 6597.
Choong Hyun Presbyterian Church (English) 665-1
Yoksam-dong, Kangnam-gu, Seoul, ph (02) 552 7270.
Yongnak Presbyterian Church (English), 69 Cho'-dong, 2-ga,
Chung-gu, Seoul, ph (02) 273 6301.
Halloelujah Christian Church (English), 908-18 Taech'i-dong,
Kangnam-gu, Seoul, ph (02) 555 9955.
International Lutheran Church (English), 726-39 Hannam-dong,
Yongsan-gu, Seoul, ph (02) 794 6274.
*Islamic*
Korea Muslim Federation (Arabic), 732 21 Hannam-dong,
Yongsan-gu, Seoul, ph (02) 794 7307.
*Buddhist*
Chogyesa Temple (Korean), 45 Kyonji-dong, Chongno-gu, Seoul,
ph (02) 735 5864.
Tosonsa Temple (Korean), 264 Ui-dong, Tobong-gu, Seoul, ph
(02) 993 3161/4.
Pongunsa Temple (Korean), 73 Samsong-dong, Kangnam-gu,
Seoul, ph (02) 545 1448.

The Saturday edition of the *Korean Times* lists the times of the
services.

# Festivals
Korea has a multitude of festivals. Many are celebrated
nationally, others are local and highlight the heritage of the
region. The chance to watch one of these festivals is a bonus for
the visitor.

### February
*Samil Folk Festival* in Yongsan. The Battle of the Bull's Heads and
Yongsan Tug of War. End of February-March.

### March
*Unsan Pyolshin Ritual* near Puyo. Honours the mountain spirit
and certain generals whose feats are part of local legend.
*Sokchonje* in Seoul to honour Confucius, his disciples and great
Korean and Chinese sages. Held twice a year in the second and

eighth lunar months in the "Hall of the Great Sages'" of Sungkyunkwan University. Usually March and September.

### April

*King Tanjong Festival* at Yongwol. A memorial ceremony for King Tanjong and his loyal ministers of the Choson Dynasty with ceremonial music and dance. Early April.

*Chinhae Cherry Blossom Festival* is held in the southern naval port of Chinhae when the cherry blossoms are in full bloom. It honours the famous Korean naval hero Admiral Yi Sun-shin, who helped defeat the Japanese invasions of 1592-98. This festival occurs in early April.

*Yongdung Festival* on Chindo Island. Celebrates a Korean version of Moses' sea-parting miracle with the Dragon King Festival, farmers' dance and a ritual to appease the spirits. Date varies.

### May

*Chohongmyo Taeje* or Royal Shrine Rites, pays homage to Choson Dynasty kings and queens. Held in Seoul at Chongmyo Shrine on the first Sunday in May. A number of royal descendants, robed in the traditional garments worn by their ancestors, take part in the rite, accompanied by court music and dance.

*Chinnam Festival* at Yosu, Chollanam-do, the headquarters of Admiral Yi Sun-shin during the Japanese invasions at the end of the 16th century. It honours Korea's greatest military hero. An archery competition and Chinese poetry writing contest highlight the festivities.

*Ch'unhyang Festival* in Namwon, Chollabuk-do, honours Ch'unhyang, a traditional Korean heroine and symbol of female virtue. P'ansori, a Korean traditional narrative song contest, is worth noting.

*Arang Festival* at Miryang. Honours Arang a Shilla, a heroine distinguished for marital fidelity. There is a beauty contest for "Miss Arang" and a ritual ceremony at Arang's Shrine. Traditional games are the highlights.

### June

*Tano Festival* in Kangnung. Kangwon-do is held to pray for a good harvest and features Shaman dances and mask drama.

*P'ungnam Festival* in Chonju is on Tano Day, the 5th day of the 5th month of the lunar calendar. A lantern parade led by a farmers' dance band threads its way from the City Hall to P'ungnammun Gate.

*Andong Folk Festival* in Andong. War of Wagons, Hanhoe mask Drama and Girls' Bridge-Crossing Games are held in the well-known historic village of Hanhoe.

## August

*Miryang Paekxhung Nori Festival* in Miryang on the 15th day of the 7th month of the lunar calendar. It features servants' festival dances, including the Yangban dance, Cripples' dance, a circle dance and a group dance. A Korean wrestling match, an archery contest and crafts sales are also held.

## October

*Mt Soraksan Festival* in Sokch'o. Commemorates the Republic of Korea's most beautiful mountain, Mt Soraksan, and the open expanses of the East Sea. Events are related to viewing the most spectacular autumn foliage and the harmony of mountain and maritime cultures.

*Chongson Arirang Festival* in Chongson. It hosts the *Arirang*, Korea's most famous folk song contest. Early October.

*Halla Festival* on Cheju-do Island, the largest and most southerly island, highlights the island's unique customs.

*King Sejong Cultural Festival* in Yoju. Honours King Sejong of the Choson Dynasty; lantern parade and circular chanting procession at Shilliksa Temple.

*Moyangsong Fortress* at Koch'and, Chollabuk-do. About 5000 women and girls tread along the fortress wall, 1680m long and 4m high, praying for long life and good health.

*Hansan Victory Festival* is held at Ch'ungmu to celebrate Admiral Yi Sun-shin's victory at Hansando Island.

*Shilla Cultural Festival* in Kyongju remembers the strength and traditions of the Shilla Kingdom with a dragon parade, processions and rituals.

*Paekche Cultural Festival* in Puyo. It honours the glory of the Paekche Kingdom Ritual processions and the flower crown dance. Venue may change.

*Kaya Cultural Festival* in Koryong celebrates the glory of the Kaya Kingdom. Kaya was one of the short-lived dynasties in southern Korea and was overshadowed by Shilla.

**November**
*Kaech'on Art Festival* at Chinju. Highlights are local cultural activities. Various Chinese poetry and calligraphy contests, music, drama performances and bullfights are held.

# Entry Regulations

All foreign visitors must have a valid passport. Visas are not required for visits of 15 days or less. Exceptions apply to countries which do not have diplomatic relations with Korea.

A certificate to say you are AIDS free may be necessary.

## Customs

Kimpo International Airport has the duel channel system. Passengers with nothing to declare may use the green channel. Prohibited articles are: books, printed matter, motion pictures, cassette tapes and other articles which are subversive to national security or harmful to public interests.

Restricted articles are: firearms, explosives and other weapons; narcotics and drugs; radio equipment (wireless transmitters, receivers and walkie-talkies); articles considered to be for commercial use; cultural property.

**Duty free allowances are**: personal clothing and toiletries; equipment and tools for direct use in your line of work; gifts to the value of W300,000; 1 bottle of liquor not exceeding 1000cc; 2oz perfume; 200 cigarettes, 50 cigars or 250gm of another tobacco product.

Articles taken out of Korea and brought back require a statement to that effect.

**Articles subject to declaration are:** More than US$5,000 or the equivalent in foreign currency; valuables to be used in Korea and taken out, such as valuable watches, cameras, golf clubs, precious metals, jewels and furs, which will be taxed on departure if not declared.

# Exit Regulations

There is a tax of W8000 on all international flights, and a domestic tax of W1000.

# Diplomatic Missions in Seoul

*Australia*: 11th floor, Kyobo Building, 1-1 Chongno 1-ga, ph (02) 730-6490/5.

*Canada*: 10th floor, Kolon Building, 45 Mugyo-dong, Chung-gu, ph (02) 753-2605/8.

*New Zealand*: 18th floor, Kyobo Building, Chongno 1-ga, Chongno-gu, ph (02) 730-7794.

*Singapore*: 7th floor, Citicorp Centre Building, 89-29 Shinmunno 2-ga, Chongno-gu, ph (02) 722-0442.

*UK*: 4 Chong-dong, Chung-gu, ph (02) 735-7341/3.

*USA*: 82 Sejongno, Chongno-gu, ph (02) 397-4114.

# Money

The unit of Korean currency is the Won (W).

Coin denominations are W1, W5, W10, W50, W100 and W500.

Bank notes are W1000, W5000 and W10,000.

Approximate exchange rates, which should be used as a guide only, are:

| | |
|---|---|
| A$1 | = 632.97W |
| Can$1 | = 591.78W |
| NZ$1 | = 559.69W |
| S$1 | = 574.07W |
| UK£1 | = 1259.64W |
| US$1 | = 805.00W |

**Major credit cards are accepted at tourist hotels, department stores and restaurants.**

It is recommended that travellers cheques be carried in US currency.

## Foreign Banks

### Australia

*ANZ*, 1.1-ga Chongno, Chongno-gu, Seoul, ph (02) 730 3151.

*National Australia Bank*, 1.1-ga, Chongno, Chongno-gu, Seoul, ph (02) 739 4600.

Westpac, 50 Sogong-dong, Chung-gu, Korea, ph (02) 756 5066.

## Canada
*Bank of Nova Scotia*, 45.1 ga Namdaemunno, Chung-gu, Seoul, ph (02) 757 7171.
*Bank of Montreal*, 88 Sogong-dong, Chongno-gu, Seoul, ph (02) 732 9206.
National Bank of Canada, 1/46-1 Susong-dong, Chongno-gu, Seoul, ph (02) 733 5012.
*Royal Bank of Canada*, 1.1-ga, Chongno, Chongno-gu, Seoul, ph (02) 730 7791.

## Singapore
Development Bank of Singapore, 1.1-ga, Chongno, Chongno-gu, Seoul, ph (02) 732 9311.
*International Bank of Singapore*, 1.1-ga, Chogno, Chogno-gu, Seoul, ph (02) 739 3441.
*Oversea-Chinese Banking Corp Ltd*, 1-170 Sunhwa-dong, Chung-gu, Seoul, ph (02) 754 4355.
*United Overseas Bank*, 1.1-ga, Chongno, Chongno-gu, Seoul, ph (02) 739 3916.

## United Kingdom
*Barclays Bank PLC*, 1-170 Sunhwa-dong, Chung-gu, Seoul, ph (02) 750 6114.
Standard Charter Bank, 9-1, 2-ga, Ulchiro, Chung-gu, Seoul, ph (02) 750 6114; 43-1 1-ga, Taech'ang-dong, Chung-gu, Pusan, ph (051) 463 6835.

## United States of America
*American Express Bank Ltd*, 64-8, 1-ga, T'aep'yongno, Chung-gu, Seoul, ph (02) 399 2929; 44-1, 2-ga, Chunung-dong, Chung-gu, Pusan, ph (051) 464 0067.
*Bank of America NT & SA*, 1, Changgyo-dong, Chung-gu, Seoul, ph (02) 729 4500; 77-1, Chungang-dong, Chung-gu, Pusan, ph (051) 462 0621.
*Bank of California NA*, 1.1-ga, Ch'ongno, Chongno-gu, Seoul, ph (02) 736 5431.
*Bank of Hawaii*, 25-5, 1-ga, Ch'ungmuro, Chung-gu, Seoul, ph (02) 757 0831.
*Bank of New York*, 250, 2-ga, T'aep'yomgno, Chung-gu, Seoul, ph (02) 774 1441; 1198-7, Ch'oryang-dong, Tong-gu, Pusan, ph (051)

465 7071.
*Banker Trust Company*, 91-1, Sogong-dong, Chung-gu, Seoul, ph (02) 311 2600.
*Chase Manhattan Bank, NA*, 34-35 Chong-dong, Chung-gu, Seoul, ph (02) 758 5114; 44, 2-ga, Chungang-dong, Chung-gu, Pusan, ph (051) 245 8073.
*Chemical Bank*, 541 Namdaemunno 5-ga, Chung-gu, Seoul, ph (02) 5411.
*Citibank NA*, 89-129 Shinmunno 2-ga, Chongno-gu, Seoul, ph (02) 731 1114; 51, 1-ga, Taech'ang-dong, Chung-gu, Pusan, ph (051) 464 3696.
*First National Bank of Boston*, 56-4, 4-ga, Chungang-dong, Chung-gu, Pusan, ph (051) 464 9991.

# National Holidays

Officially Koreans follow the Gregorian calendar of the Orient.

During the holidays, offices and banks are closed. Palaces, museums, most restaurants and amusement facilities are open. Taxis and other transport are available.

*New Years Day* - January 1 and 2. Members of the family rise early, don their best clothes and bow to their elders as a reaffirmation of family ties.

*Lunar New Year*. New Years Day by the lunar calendar is called Sol. It is the second most important holiday. Families carry out ceremonies to commemorate their ancestors. Various traditional games are played. Date is moveable.

*Independence Movement Day*. Koreans observe the anniversary of the March 1, 1919 Independence Movement against Japanese colonial rule. The ceremony features an annual reading of the Korean Proclamation of Independence.

*Arbor Day* - April 5. Trees are planted all across the country as part of the nation's vast re-forestation program.

*Children's Day* - May 5. It is celebrated with various programs for children. Parks and children's centres are packed with colourfully dressed boys and girls.

*Buddha's Birthday.* The 8th day of the 4th lunar month (usually in May). It is also called "Feast of the Lanterns". Elaborate and solemn rituals are held at many Buddhist temples while lanterns are displayed in temple courtyards. In the evening, the lanterns are carried in parades.

*Constitution Day* - July 17. This holiday commemorates the proclamation of the constitution on July 17, 1948.

*Liberation Day* - August 15. It commemorates the Japanese acceptance of the Allied terms of surrender in 1945.

*Ch'usok.* The 15th day of the 8th lunar month (September). It is the greatest holiday of the year. It is referred to as the Korean Thanksgiving Day. People visit family tombs and make offerings to their ancestors.

*National Foundation Day* - October 3. It commemorates the founding of the Korean nation, the Ko-Choson Kingdom 2333BC.

*Christmas Day* - December 25. Christmas is observed as a national holiday in Korea as in most parts of the world.

## Communications

South Korea has 30 daily papers. Two English language dailies are *The Korean Times* and *The Korean Herald* and they are obtainable from most news-stands and hotel shops. There are four television networks, with all programs in Korean. There is also the American Forces Korea network operated by the US military. Reception outside the Seoul area is not always good.

There are eight radio stations, plus the US military station which broadcasts in English.

### Mail

Domestic postal rates are W110 for a letter up to 50g.
**Aerograms cost W350 and Airmail letters up to 10g range from W370 for Far East Asia to W470 for Latin America and Africa.**
Telegrams can be phoned through or written out at the Post Office. If written in English the cost is W80 per word.

International rates for postcards vary from W240 to Hong Kong, W660 to Australia W610 to UK and W280 to USA.

### Telephone

Korea has IDD facilities and the country code is 82.

There are three types of public telephone in Korea - blue, grey and card.

Grey and blue phones can be used for both local and long distance calls. A local call costs W30 for three minutes. Long distance calls cost considerably more, and time can be extended by depositing more money. These telephones take W10, W50 and W100 coins.

Card telephones can be used for international as well as local and long distance calls. Cards come in W2000, W3000, W5000 and W10,000 units. They are on sale at shops close to the telephone boxes and at banks.

There are two international access codes in Korea - 001 and 002. The latter offers a rate that is 5% cheaper than the former.

International calls can also made through the operator by dialling 0077, and collect calls can be made by dialling 007. For international call information dial 0074.

Always remember that it is cheaper to use a public phone than the one in your hotel room.

# Tourist Information

Information for visitors is readily available at the **Korean National Tourist Corporation (KNTC)** centres. The main office is at B1, KNTC Building, 10, Ta-dong, Chung-gu, Seoul, ph (02) 757 0086. Among its facilities are an information desk, relief maps, a theatrette, and travellers' phone service. It is open daily 9am-6pm (March-October), 9am-5pm (November-February).

### Other offices are located at:

Hotel Lotte, 1 Sogong-dong, Chung-gu, Seoul, ph (02) 771 1000.

Kimpo Airport, 1st floor, Airport Terminal Buildings 1 & 2, Seoul, ph (02) 665 008/0986.

Kimhae Airport Information Centre, 210, Taejo 2-dong, Puk-gu, Pusan, ph (051) 973 1100.

Cheju Airport Information Centre, 2096 Yongdam-dong, Cheju, ph (064) 42 0032.

The Seoul metropolitan authorities also operate the **Seoul Tourist Information Centre** directly behind the City Hall, at 31, T'aep'yongno-1-ga, Chung-gu, Seoul, ph (02) 731 6337, 731 6737, 735 8688. It is open every day 9am-6pm (March-October), 9am-5pm (November-February). They also operate information counters at major locations that are open Mon-Fri 9am-4pm, Sat 9am-3pm.

Other information centres are: Chongno-5-ga, ph (02) 272 0348; It'aewon, ph (02) 794 2490; Kwanghwamun, ph (02) 735 0088; Myong-dong, ph (02) 757 0088; Pagoda Park, ph (02) 739 4331; Seoul Express Bus Terminal, ph (02) 537 9198; and Toksugung Palace, ph (02) 756 0046.

## Miscellaneous

**Tipping is not a traditional Korean custom.** A 10% service charge is added to the bill at all tourist hotels. It is not necessary to tip a taxi driver unless he assists you with luggage or provides an extra service.

Police boxes can be found on every major street.

Identification - carry your passport with you and a driving licence if you have one.

Emergency Phone Numbers - dial 112 for police, 119 for fire brigade. Your hotel will arrange for a doctor or ambulance. Asia Emergency Assistance for foreigners (02) 790-7561 has a 24-hour service acting as a link with the patient and Korean hospitals, for a fee.

Electricity is 110-220 volt. Travellers should take an international adaptor.

Korea uses the Metric system for weights and measures.

### Time zone
When it is 1pm in Seoul it is:
    2pm in Sydney
    4am in London

4pm in Auckland
noon in Singapore
11pm in New York (previous day).
7.30pm in Vancouver (previous day).

## Opening Times
Banks are open Mon-Fri 9.30am-4.30pm; Sat 9.30am-1.30pm.
Small shops are open almost all the time.
Department stores are open daily 10.30am-7.30pm including Sundays. Foreign Diplomatic Missions are open Mon-Fri 9am-5pm.
Government office hours are Mon-Fri 9am-6pm; Sat 9am-1pm.

## Water
It is advisable to buy bottled water. Your hotel may supply purified water in a thermos or in bottles if there is a refrigerator in the room.

## Health
No vaccinations are necessary. However, protection from yellow fever and cholera are recommended for those travelling from an infected country.

## Complaints
Should a visitor wish to complain about an experience or inconvenience, they should call or write to the Tourist Complaint Centre, GPO Box 903, Seoul, 100-609, ph (02) 735-0101.

## Lost and Found
If any property is lost or left on public transport contact the Citizens Room of Seoul Metropolitan Police Bureau, 20-11, Naeja-dong, Vhung-gu, ph (02) 725 4400.

## Value Added Tax (VAT)
This is levied on most goods and services at a standard rate of 10%. In tourist hotels the 10% is charged on rooms, meals and other services and added to the bill.

### *Etiquette*

In Korea, the traditional Confucian social structure, although changing, is prevalent. Age seniority is all important and juniors are expected to follow the wishes of their elders without question. You will quite often be asked your age and possibly your marital status. This is not meant personally but simply to find out their relative position to you. Married people have a slightly higher status within society. You do not have to answer.

Greetings and thanks are very important to Koreans. Words are always said with a bow of the head.

Koreans do not appreciate an overly outgoing style. They limit direct physical contact to a handshake. However, foreigners are often quite surprised to see men, especially young men, walking in the street with their arms around each other's shoulders or women walking hand in hand.

Touching close friends while talking to them is acceptable. Public kissing and hugging tend to be regarded as unseemly.

Public conveniences are few in Korea. It is totally admissible to use those in office blocks, hotels, shops and restaurants.

Koreans traditionally eat, sleep and sit on the floor, so shoes should be removed before entering a Korean house. It is best to wear socks or pantyhose.
There is no such thing as paying 'Dutch' to Koreans. Visitors should act as guest or host.

It is impolite to talk too much during meals. Appreciation of food and service is gratefully received. It is impolite to blow one's nose at the dinner table.

# Travel Information

## How to get There

### By Air

Korea is located close to many major Asian cities, and flight connections can be made easily from all parts of the world. Major international airlines have about 480 scheduled direct or non-stop flights per week between Seoul and major cities in Asia, America, Europe, Australia, North Africa and the Middle East.

International airlines maintaining regular flight services to Korea are listed below.

The phone numbers given are for their offices in Seoul.

*Aeroflot (SU),*          ph (02) 551 0321/4.
*Air China (CA),*          ph (02) 518 0330.
*Air France (AF),*          ph (02) 773 3151
*Air New Zealand (NZ),*          ph (02) 777 6626
*Alitalia (AZ),*          ph (02) 779 1676/6
*All Nippon (NH),*          ph (02) 752 5500
*Asiana Korean (OZ),*          ph (02) 774 4000
*British Airways (BA),*          ph (02) 774 5511
*Cathay Pacific (CX),*          ph (02) 773 0321/6
*China Eastern Airlines (MU),* ph (02) 518 0330
*Continental Airlines (CO),*  ph (02) 773 0100
*Delta Airlines (DL),*          ph (02) 754 1921
*Garuda (GA),*          ph (02) 773 2092/3
*Japan Airlines (JL),*          ph (02) 757 1720
*Japan Air System (JD),*          ph (02) 752 9090/1
*Korean Air (KE),*          ph (02) 756 2000
*Lufthansa German Airlines (LH),* ph (02) 538 8141/3
*Malaysian Airlines (MH),*  ph (02) 777 7761/2
*Nippon Cargo (NW),*          ph (02) 775 3921/4
*Northwest Airlines (NW),*  ph (02) 734 7800

*Philippine Airlines (PR),*   ph (02) 774 3581/4
*Qantas Airways (QF),*   ph (02) 777 6871/3
*KLM Royal Dutch Airlines (KL),* ph (02) 753 1093
*Singapore Airlines (SQ),*   ph (02) 755 1226/8
*Swiss Air (SR),*   ph (02) 757 8901
*Thai Airways International (TG),* ph (02) 754 9960
*United Airlines (UA),*   ph (02) 757 1691
*Vietnam Airlines (VN),*   ph (02) 775 5477/8.

### By Sea

Pusan is South Korea's largest port. Visitors arriving by ship come mainly from Japan. The Pukwan, Kuk Jae, Korea and the Korea Marine express ferry companies have regular services between Korea and Japan. The Weidong and Tianjin ferry companies have regular services to China. There is a hydrofoil service between Pusan and Shimonseki, and Pusan and Hakata.

Temporary entry is allowed for private cars belonging to all visitors arriving by ferry providing that each owner has proper documentation for the car.

There is a Korea-Japan through ticket which enables the holder to travel to or from Korea and Japan by train, taking the ferry crossing between Pusan and Shimonoseki.

The system is jointly operated by Aju Travel Service, Korea and Nippon Travel Agency, Japan.

## Package Tours

There are plenty of package tours available from Australia, England, USA, Germany, Japan, Hong Kong and many other countries. There are even some to North Korea but they have to be taken from Beijing or Bangkok.

The tours cover the major highlights of the country and for those who wish to avoid language problems, they are highly recommended.

## Transport from the Airport

*Airport Express Buses* link Kimpo International Airport and Downtown Seoul. There are three bus lines: No 600 runs south of the Hangang River departing every seven minutes; No 600-2 runs between the airport and the Express terminal along the same route and operates every 20 minutes; and No 601 runs between the airport and the Eastern Hotel, via the city centre north of the river, every 10 minutes. The one-way fare is W650.

*Kai Limousine* luxury buses seat 25, are equipped with public phones and radio, and operate between the airport and 19 luxury hotels. They return on each route every 20-30 minutes. The one-way fare is W3500. Tickets are available at airport terminals or hotel desks. Tickets should be purchased before boarding. Videos in English, Korean and Japanese featuring major tourist attractions, are played on board.

*Airport Limousine* non-stop buses are the most convenient form of transport for those with heavy luggage. The bus leaves the airport every 10-15 minutes. Travel time is about one hour. The fare is W2000 one way and tickets can be bought in the terminals or on the bus itself.

# Local Transport

### Air

*Korean Air* and *Asiana Airlines* service the domestic flight network, linking Korea's 14 major cities. Flight time to any of these destinations, including Chejudo Island, is around one hour.

Reservations can be made by calling one of the airline offices listed below. KNTC operates a ticket sales outlet at KNTC Building, 10 Ta-dong, Chung-gu, Seoul, ph (02) 753 9870.

| Reservation Offices | Korean Air | Asiana Air |
|---|---|---|
| Seoul | (02) 756 2000 | (02) 774 4000 |
| Pusan | (051) 463 2000 | (051) 465 4000 |
| Cheju | (064) 52 2000 | (064) 43 4000 |
| Kwangju | (062) 222 2000 | (062) 226 4000 |
| Taegu | (053) 423 2000 | (053) 421 4000 |
| Yosu | (0662) 41 2000 | (0662) 652 4000 |
| Sokch'o | (0392) 32 2000 | |
| Chinju | (0591) 57 2000 | (0591) 758 4000 |
| Ulsan | (0522) 71 2000 | (0522) 61 4000 |
| Kangnung | (0391) 43 2000 | |
| P'ohang | (0562) 72 2000 | (0562) 77 4000 |
| Yech'on | (0584) 54 4000 | |
| Mokp'o | (0631) 73 2000 | (0631) 78 4000 |
| Kunsan | (0654) 471 2000. | |

They expect travellers to use credit cards so make sure you have one ready.

## Bus
*Long Distance Express Buses*
Fast and reliable express highway bus services operate throughout the country to almost all major points. There are two express terminals in Seoul.

The Seoul Express Bus Terminal is the main depot for trips out of Seoul. It is conveniently served by the Express Bus Terminal Underground Station on line 3. Tong Seoul Express Bus Terminal also called Ku-ui, is adjacent to Kangbyon Underground station on line 2.

The Seoul Express Terminal is divided into two separate buildings. The Kyongbuson terminal services Pusan and several cities along the route including historic Kyongju. The Honam-Yongdongson terminal covers cities on the east coast and south-western provinces.

*Intercity Buses*
Korea has excellent intercity bus services connecting virtually all the cities and towns. Since there are no English language schedules available, it is advisable for a foreign traveller to take along a Korean friend.

## Train
Passenger trains operated by the Korean National Railway, are reasonably fast, reliable and moderately priced. An extensive network covers almost every part of the country.

There are four classes of trains: super-express *Saemaul-ho,* limited express *Mungunghwa-ho,* express *T'ongil-ho,* and ordinary trains *Bidulgi-ho.* The fastest and most comfortable are the super-express. The coaches are heated in winter and air-conditioned in summer. They also have private compartments for families or groups. For most destinations, trains are full at weekends and holidays. Advance reservation and purchase are recommended. Tickets are obtainable from most tourist agencies and the government-run Korean Travel Bureau, which has two offices. One is at 1465-11 Soch'o 3-dong, Soch'o-gu, Seoul, ph (02) 585 1191, fax (02) 585 1187; the other is in the Hotel Lotte.

There are also ticket counters for foreigners at some major stations.

### Ferry
Boat travel is one of the most pleasant ways to journey around Korea. Ships ply between Pusan and Cheju, Mokp'o and Homgdo, P'ohang and Ullungdo, etc. There is also a hydrofoil that runs between Pusan and Yosu calling at Ch'ungmu on the way. The scenic cruise winding in and out of the islands within the Hallyosudo Waterway is gaining in popularity with visitors.

### Han-Gang River Cruise
The Han-Gang River meanders through the heart of the nation and passes through Seoul. There are many scenic attractions along the banks and it is a must for visitors to Seoul. There are six different cruise courses, each lasting about an hour. Ring Semo Company on (02) 785-4411.

# City Transport

### Bus
The bus systems differ slightly from city to city. This is a brief explanation of the Seoul system. There are two types, city and express, and they are everywhere and numbered according to routes. As the signs are written in Korean, finding the right bus can be quite confusing. Ask one of the hotel staff to write down the number and destination of the bus you want and tell you where to catch it.

Local city buses are the most common means of transport. They are frequent, reliable and cheap. The fare is W250 by token regardless of distance. Tokens can be bought from booths near most stops. If you pay on the bus the fare is W260. These buses are often crowded and have only a single row of seats on each side. All buses are marked with numbers and signs in blue and red on the front, side and rear indicating their routes and stops in the city.

City Express buses, called *chwasok* in Korean, are more comfortable than the local buses and are air-conditioned in summer. They stop less often and are only supposed to pick up the number of passengers for which they have seats. The fare is W550.

### The Underground
More often called the subway, this is the most efficient and convenient method of transport for foreign visitors. Ticket

windows, station names and transfer signs are all clearly marked in English as well as Korean. Four lines serve Seoul and a colour system is used for routing. The underground has automatic ticket barriers and is clean and effective. One-way tickets to most places inside the city are W300.

You will find shopping arcades in many of the underground passageways. These go for miles and have some of the best shopping in the city.

## Car Rental
Driving safely in Korea takes some practice due to the different traffic laws, so it is advisable to hire a driver with the car. Of course the rates then rise to include accommodation and meals for the chauffeur. The cost for a 10-hour day is W50,000.

## Taxis
Taxis are plentiful and reasonably priced, and there are taxi stands throughout the city. They can also be hailed on the street or you can phone for one but the fare will then be much higher.

The usual taxi is a grey sedan. Fares are W900 for the first 2km with W100 for each additional 381m. The fare system is based on distance and time taken. If a taxi is going at less than 15km per hour, an additional charge of W100 is made for every 92 seconds. The fare from Kimpo Airport to downtown Seoul is around W12,500, but this depends on traffic.

*Deluxe Taxis* are black with a yellow sign on top and the words "deluxe taxi" written on the sides. They offer a high standard of service. Fares are W3000 for the first 3km and W200 for each additional 250m or 60 seconds if the speed drops below 15km per hour. The usual fare between Kimpo and downtown Seoul is W23,000-35,000. Receipts are given and there is no late night surcharge. Deluxe taxis can only be taken from their stands located at hotels, stations, bus terminals and on major city streets.

Do not presume that taxi drivers speak English. Some do, but ask your hotel to tell the driver where you want to go or ask them to write it down in Korean.

# Accommodation

There are many modern hotels in the major tourist destinations. Tourist hotels are registered with the government and classified according to size, quality and facilities available.

**There are five groups:**
**super deluxe, deluxe, first class, second class and third class.**
The Rose of Sharon, Korea's national flower, is used as a symbol of quality. 10% VAT is charged on rooms, meals and services plus a 10% service charge. Tipping is not required. It is advisable to pay a little more for your accommodation to ensure that those in reception, the cashier and the hall porter speak English. You do not have to stay in one of the deluxe hotels, which are very expensive, but first class would be advised. It is important that your travel agent double checks this. Also look at a map to see where the hotel is situated. If a taxi is required to reach shops and attractions, this will add to your costs.

Following is a list of hotels, with prices for a double room per night, which should be used as a guide only.

## Seoul

### Super Deluxe Hotels

*Hilton International*, 395 Namdaemunno 5-ga, Chung-gu, ph (02) 753-7788 - 698 rooms - restaurant, cocktail bar, indoor pool, night club, health club, sauna - W160,000 (US$251).
*Lotte*, 1 Sogong-dong, Chung-gu, ph (02) 771-1000 - 1482 rooms - restaurant, cocktail bar, health club, indoor pool, night club, sauna - W145,000-195,000 (US$227-306).
*Seoul Renaissance*, 676 Yoksam-dong, Kangnam-gu, ph (02) 555-0501 - 493 rooms - restaurant, cocktail bar, health club, indoor pool, night club, sauna, tennis court - W155,000-190,000 (US$243-298).

*Westin Choson*, 87 Sogong-dong, Chung-gu, ph (02) 771-0500
- 477 rooms - restaurant, cocktail bar, health club, outdoor pool -
W145,000-192,000 (US$228-300).

*Plaza*, 23 T'aep'yongno 2-ga, Chung-gu, ph (02) 771-2200 - 496
rooms - restaurant, cocktail bar, health club, sauna - W140,000
(US$220).

*Lotte World*, 40-1 Chamshil-dong, Songp'a-gu, ph (02)
419-7000 - 495 rooms - restaurant, cocktail bar, health club, sauna -
W140,000 (US$220).

*Shilla*, 202 Changch'ung-dong 2-ga, Chung-gu, ph (02)
233-3131 - 598 rooms - restaurant, cocktail bar, night club, health
club, indoor pool, outdoor pool, sauna - W137,000-290,000
(US$215-455).

*Grand Hyatt*, 747-7 Hannnam-dong, Yongsan-gu, ph (02)
797-1234 - 596 rooms - restaurant, night club, cocktail bar, indoor &
outdoor pools, health club, sauna - W135,000 (US$212).

Intercontinental, 159-8 Samsong-dong, Kangnam-gu, ph (02)
555-5656 - 596 rooms - restaurant, cocktail bar, night club, indoor
pool, health club, sauna - W135,000-152,000 (US$212-238).

*Sheraton Walker Hill*, San-21 Kwangjang-dong, Songdong-gu, ph
(02) 453-0121 - 615 rooms - restaurant, theatre restaurant, casino,
night club, cocktail bar, health club, indoor & outdoor pools, sauna,
tennis court - W120,000-165,000 (US$188-259).

*Swiss Grand*, 201-1 Hongun-dong, Sodaemun-gu, ph (02) 356-56565
- 397 rooms - restaurant, cocktail bar, night club, health club, indoor
pool, sauna - W110,000-125,000 (US$172-196).

### Deluxe Hotels

*New World*, 112-5 Samsong-dong, Kangnam-gu, ph (02) 557-0111
- 209 rooms - restaurant, cocktail bar, health club, indoor pool,
sauna - W112,500 (US$176).

*Sofitel Ambassador*, 186-54 Changch'ung-dong 2-ga, Chung-gu, ph
(02) 275-1101 - 440 rooms - restaurant, theatre restaurant, cocktail
bar, night club, sauna - W112,500 (US$176).

*Capital*, 22-76 It'aewon-dong, Yongsan-gu, ph (02) 792-1122 - 274
rooms - restaurant, night club, cocktail bar, health club, indoor
pool, sauna, tennis court - W110,000 (US$172).

*Emerald*, 129 Ch'ongdam-dong, Kangnam-gu, ph (02) 514-3535
- 121 rooms - restaurant, cocktail bar, health club, sauna - W110,000
(US$172).

*Seoul Palace*, 63-1 Panp'o-dong, Soch'o-gu, ph (02) 532-5000 - 265 rooms - restaurant, night club, cocktail bar, health club, sauna - W106,000 (US$166).

*Riviera*, 53-7 Ch'ongdam-dong, Kangnam-gu, ph (02) 541-3111 - 146 rooms - restaurant, night club, cocktail bar, health club, indoor pool, sauna - W105,000 (US$165).

*Garden*, 169-1 Tohwa-dong, Map'o-gu, ph (02) 717-9441 - 386 rooms - restaurant, night club, cocktail bar, health club, indoor pool, sauna - W105,000 (US$165).

*King Sejong*, 61-3 Ch'ungmuro 2-ga, Chung-gu, (02) 776-1811 - 227 rooms - restaurant, cocktail bar, health club, sauna - W104,500-110,700 (US$164-174).

*Tower*, San 5-51 Changchh'ung-dong 2-ga, Chung-gu, ph (02) 236-2121 - 188 rooms - restaurant, nightclub, cocktail bar, health club, outdoor pool, sauna, tennis courts - W103,000 (US$162).

*Royal* 6 Myong-dong 1-ga, Chung-gu, ph (02) 756-1112 - 302 rooms - restaurant, night club, cocktail bar, sauna - W103,500-112,500 (US$162-176).

*President*, 188-3 Ulchiro 1-ga, Chung-gu, ph (02) 753-3131 - 295 rooms - restaurant, cocktail bar - W101,500 (US$159).

*Ramada Olympia*, 108-2 P'yongch'ang-dong, Chongno-gu, ph (02) 353-5121 - 286 rooms - restaurant, night club, theatre restaurant, cocktail bar, health club, indoor & outdoor pools, sauna - W100,000 (US$156).

*Koreana*, 61-1 T'aep'yongno 1-ga, Chung-gu, ph (02) 730-9911 - 277 rooms - restaurant, cocktail bar - W97,000-103,500 (US$152-162).

*Riverside*, 6-1 Chamwon-dong, Sch'o-gu, ph (02) 543-1001 - 157 rooms - restaurant, night club, cocktail bar, health club, indoor pool, sauna - W97,000 (US$152

### First Class Hotels

*Amiga*, 248-7 Nonhyon-dong, Kangnam-gu, ph (02) 511-4000 - 101 rooms - restaurant, cocktail bar, tennis court - W112,500 (US$176).

*Manhattan*, 13-3 Youido-dong, Yongdungp'o-gu, ph (02) 780-8001 - 174 rooms - restaurant, night club, cocktail bar, health club, sauna - W90,000 (US$141).

*New Seoul*, 29-1 T'aep'yong-no 1-ga, Chung-gu, ph (02) 735-9071 - 129 rooms - restaurant, cocktail bar, sauna - W70,000 (US$110).

Holiday It'aewon, 737-32 Hannam-dong, Yongsan-guy, ph (02) 792-3111 - 118 rooms - restaurant, night club, cocktail bar - W68,500

(US$107).
*Dong Seoul*, 595 Kuui-dong, Songdong-gu, ph (02) 455-1100 - 93 rooms
- restaurant, night club, cocktail bar, sauna - W68,500 (US$107).
Seokyo, 354-5 Sogyo-dong, Map'o-gu, ph (02) 333-7771 - 99 rooms -
restaurant, night club, cocktail bar, health club, indoor pool, sauna -
W68,500 (US$107).
*Hamilton*, 119-25 It'aewon-dong, Yongsan-gu, ph (02) 794-0171
- 136 rooms - restaurant, night club, outdoor pool - W68,500
(US$107).
*Prima*, 52-3 Ch'ongdam-dong, Kangnam-gu, ph (02)
549-9011 - 83 rooms - restaurant, cocktail bar, sauna - W68,500
(US$107).
*Moksan*, 454-2 Ch'onho-dong, Kangdong-gu, ph (02)
470-5002 - 94 rooms - restaurant, night club, cocktail bar, sauna -
W68,000 (US$106).
*New Star*, 24 Sokch'on-dong, Songp'a-gu, ph (02) 420-0100 - 46
rooms - restaurant, cocktail bar, sauna - W68,000 (US$106).
*Green Grass*, 141-10 Samsong-dong, Kangnam-gu, ph (02)
555-7575 - 52 rooms - restaurant, night club, cocktail bar - W67,000
(US$105).
*Pacific*, 31-1 Namsan-dong 2-ga, Chung-gu, ph (02) 777-7811
- 111 rooms - restaurant, night club, theatre restaurant, cocktail bar,
sauna - W64,600 (US$101).
*Crown*, 34-69 It'aewon-dong, Yongsan-gu, ph (02) 797-4111 - 154
rooms - restaurant, night club, sauna - W60,000 (US$94).
Samjung, 604-11 Yoksam-dong, Kangnam-gu, ph (02) 557-1221
- 154 rooms - restaurant, night club, cocktail bar, sauna - W60,000
(US$94).
*Victoria*, 42-8 Mia 4-dong, Tobong-gu, ph (02) 986-2000 - 63 rooms -
restaurant, night club, theatre restaurant, health club, indoor pool,
sauna - W60,000 (US$94).
*Kyungnam*, 366-7 Changan-dong, Tongdaemun-gu, ph (02) 247-2500
- 94 rooms - restaurant, night club, cocktail bar, sauna - W60,000
(US$94).
*Poongjun*, 73-1 Inhyon-dong, Chung-gu, ph (02) 266-2151 - 167
rooms - restaurant, night club, cocktail bar - W60,000 (US$86).
*Seo Seoul*, 381-17 Hapchong-dong, Map'o-gu, ph (02)
332-1122 - 70 rooms - restaurant, cocktail bar, sauna - W55,000
(US$86).
*Youngdong*, 6 Nonhyon-dong, Kangnam-gu, ph (02)
542-0112 - 136 rooms - restaurant, night club, theatre restaurant,

cocktail bar, sauna - W55,300 (US$86).

Aroma, 505-23 Tungch'on-dong, Kangso'gu, ph (02) 653-1999 - 47 rooms - restaurant, night club, cocktail bar, health club, sauna - W50,000 (US$78).

### Second Class Hotels

*Hilltop,* 151-30 Nonhyon-dong, Kangnam-gu, ph (02) 540-3451 - 49 rooms - restaurant, night club, cocktail bar, health club, sauna - W65,000 (US$102).

*New Hilltop,* 152 Nonhyon-dong, Kangnam-gu, ph (02) 540-1121 - 58 rooms - cocktail bar, health club - W57,850 (US$90).

*Hankang,* 188-2 Kwangjang-dong, Songdong-gu, ph (02) 453-5131 - 74 rooms - restaurant, night club, cocktail bar - W48,400 (US$76).

River Park, 260 Yomch'ang-dong, Kangso-gu, ph (02) 653-3000 - 35 rooms - restaurant, cocktail bar - W46,000 (US$72).

*Regent,* 1111-7 Hwagok-dong, Songp'a-gu, ph (02) 421-2131 - 42 rooms - sauna - W46,000 (US$72).

Marguerite, 3-1343 Chongam-dong, Songbuk-gu, ph (02) 929-2000 - 58 rooms - restaurant, night club, theatre restaurant - W45,000 (US$70).

*Las Vegas,* 94-154 Yongdungp'o 2-ga, Yongdungp'o-gu, ph (02) 675-7321 - 43 rooms - restaurant, sauna - W42,975 (US$67).

*Brown,* 77-2 Pomun-dong, Songbuk-gu, ph (02) 926-6601 - 39 rooms - restaurant, cocktail bar - W38,100 (US$60).

*Clover,* 129-7 Ch'ongdam-dong, Kangnam-gu, ph (02) 546-1411 - 51 rooms - restaurant, night club, cocktail bar, sauna - W38,100 (US$60).

*Kims,* 66-50 P'yongch'ang-dong, Chongno-gu, ph (02) 357-0520 - 43 rooms - restaurant, cocktail bar - W38,100 (US$60).

*Mirabeau,* 104-36 Taehyon-dong, Sodaemun-gu, ph (02) 392-9511 - 45 rooms - restaurant, cocktail bar - W38,100 (US$60).

*New Star Kimpo,* 1110 Hwagok-dong, Kangso-gu, ph (02) 691-0071 - 53 rooms - restaurant, night club, cocktail bar - W38,100 (US$60).

*Dynasty,* 202-7 Nonhyon-dong, Kangnam-gu, ph (02) 540-3041 - 44 rooms - restaurant, cocktail bar - W38,100 (US$60).

Jamsil, 250-9 Chamshil-dong, Songp'a-gu, ph (02) 421-2761 - 44 rooms - restaurant, cocktail bar - W38,100 (US$60).

*Kingdom,* 366-144 Shindang-dong, Chung-gu, ph (02) 237-5181 - 44 rooms - restaurant, night club, cocktail bar, health club, sauna - W38,000 (US$60).

*Sunshine*, 587-1 Shinsa-dong, Kangnam-gu, ph (02) 541-1818 - 80 rooms - restaurant, cocktail bar, sauna - W38,000 (US$60).

*Han Yang*, 302-13 Pulkwang-dong, Unp'yong-gu, ph (02) 352-3131 - 68 rooms - restaurant, night club, cocktail bar, sauna - W38,000 (US$60).

*Savoy*, 23-1 Ch'ungmuro 1-ga, Chung-gu, (02) 776-2641 - 98 rooms - cocktail bar - W36,000-38,000 (US$56-60).

*Yoido*, 10-3 Youido-dong, Yongdungp'o-gu, ph (02) 782-0121 86 rooms - restaurant, night club, cocktail bar - W36,777 (US$57).

*Green Park San*, 14 Ui-dong, Tobong-gu, ph (02) 900-8181 - 75 rooms - restaurant, cocktail bar, outdoor pool, tennis court - W36,000 (US$56).

*Seoul Prince*, 1-1 Namsan-dong 2-ga, Chung-gu, ph (02) 752-7111 - 87 rooms - restaurant - W35,000-38,000 (US$55-60).

City Palace, 497-23 Tapshimni 5-dong, Tomgdaemun-gu, ph (02) 244-2222 - 37 rooms - restaurant, theatre restaurant, cocktail bar, sauna - W35,000 (US$55).

*Seoul*, 92 Ch'ongin-dong, Chongno-gu, ph (02) 735-9001 - 86 rooms - restaurant, cocktail bar, sauna - W33,000-47,000 (US$52-73).

*Metro*, 199-33 Ulchiro 2-ga, Chung-gu, ph (02) 752-1112 - 79 rooms - restaurant, cocktail bar - W33,000-38,000 (US$52-60)

*New Orientaal*, 10 Hoehyon-dong, Chung-gu, ph (02) 753-0701 - 79 rooms - cocktail bar - W33,000 (US$52).

## *Third Class Hotels*

Karak, 98-5 Karak-dong, Songp'a-gu, ph (02) 400-6641 - 36 rooms - night club, sauna - W42,000 (US$65).

*Hyejeon* 146-4 Samsong-dong, Kangnam-gu, ph (02) 546-0225 - 43 rooms - cocktail bar - W42,000 (US$65).

*Central*, 227-1 Changsa-dong, Chongno-gu, ph (02) 962-0021 - 64 rooms - restaurant, night club, cocktail bar - W40,000 (US$62).

*L.A.*, 417-5 Dongnae-dong, Kangdong-gu, ph (02) 484-2871 - 31 rooms - restaurant, cocktail bar - W39,000 (US$61).

*Eastern*, 444-14 Ch'angshin-dong, Chongno-gu, ph (02) 741-7811 - 44 rooms - night club, sauna - W37,000 (US$58).

Boolim, 602-27 Chonnong 2-dong, Tongdaemun-gu, ph (02) 962-0021 - 51 rooms - restaurant, night club - W36,300 (US$57).

*Yongdungpo*, 33-10 Tangsan-dong 5-ga, Yongdungp'o-gu, (02) 678-4265 45 rooms - Bed only W35,200 (US$55).

*Giant*, 45-10 Samsong-dong, Kangnam-gu, ph (02) 546-0225 - 47 rooms - restaurant, night club, cocktail bar, sauna - W35,000 (US$55).

*Samhwa*, 527-3 Shinsa-dong, Kangnam-gu, ph (02) 541-1011 - 45 rooms - restaurant - W35,000 (US$55).

*Astoria*, 13-2 Namhak-dong, Chung-gu, ph (02) 268-7111 - 77 rooms - restaurant, cocktail bar - W35,000 (US$55).

*Sofia*, 88-1 Ssangmun-dong, Tobong-gu, ph (02) 900-8011 -45 rooms - restaurant, cocktail bar, sauna - W40,000 (US$63).

*Alps*, 365-8 Changan-dong, Tongdaemun-gu, ph (02) 248-1161 - 42 rooms - cocktail bar, night club - W35,000 (US$55).

*Ruby*, 1605-7 Soch'o-dong, Soch'o-gu, ph (02) 521-7113 - 34 rooms - restaurant, cocktail bar - W35,000 (US$55).

*Rio*, 72-7 Kwanghui-dong, 1-ga Chung-gu, ph (02) 278-5700 - 52 rooms - restaurant, cocktail bar, sauna - W35,000 (US$55).

*Sangwon*, 33 Nakwon-dong, Chongno-gu, ph (02) 752-3191 - 60 rooms - restaurant, cocktail bar - W32,000 (US$50).

*Samho*, 436-73 Ch'angshin-dong, Chongno-gu, ph (02) 741-7080 - 43 rooms - sauna - W32,000 (US$50).

*YMCA*, 9 Chogno 2-ga, Chongno-gu, ph (02) 732-8291 - 79 rooms - restaurant - W31,500 (US$49).

*Kaya*, 98-11 Kalwol-dong, Yongsan-gu, ph (02) 798-5101 - 42 rooms - night club, sauna - W31,405 (US$49).

*Jeonpoong*, 58-1 Toson-dong, Songdong-gu, ph (02) 295-9365 - 32 rooms - restaurant, night club - W30,000 (US$50).

Sangbong Newstar, 90-3 Sangbong-dong, Chungnang-gu, ph (02) 496-6111 - 36 rooms - restaurant, sauna - W26,900 (US$42).

*Airport*, 11-21 Konghang-dong, Kangso-gu, ph (02) 662-1113 - 41 rooms - sauna - W25,000 (US$39).

*Chonji*, 133-1 Ulchiro 5-ga, Chung-gu, ph (02) 265-6131 - 61 rooms - restaurant, night club, cocktail bar, sauna - W25,000 (US$39).

## Pusan

### Super Deluxe Hotels

*Paradise Beach*, 1408-5 Chung-dong, Haeundae-gu, ph (051) 742-2121 - 234 rooms - restaurant, night club, cocktail bar, health club, outdoor pool, sauna, tennis court - W107,000-145,000 (US$168-227).

*Hyatt Regency*, 1405-16 Chung-dong, Haeundae-gu, ph (051) 743-1234 - 355 rooms - restaurant, theatre restaurant, night club, cocktail bar, health club, indoor pool, sauna, tennis court -W102,000-123,000 (US$160-193).

*Westin Chosun Beach*, 737.U 1-dong, Haeundae-gu, ph (051)

742-7411 - 289 rooms - restaurant, cocktail bar, health club, indoor pool, sauna - W102,000-123,000 (US$160-193).

## Deluxe Hotels
*Sorabol* 37-1.1-ga, Taech'ong-dong, Chung-gu, ph (051) 463-3511/19 - 152 rooms - restaurant, cocktail bar, sauna - W63,300 (US$99).
*Commodore* 743-80 Yongju-dong, Chung-gu, ph (051) 466-9101/7 - 316 rooms - restaurant, night club, cocktail bar, health club, indoor pool, sauna - W61,300-67,200 (US$96-105).

## First Class Hotels
*Gwangajung*, 1509-2 Chung-dong, Haeundae-gu, ph (051) 744-1331 - 40 rooms - restaurant, cocktail bar - W56,660 (US$89).
*Royal*, 2-72 Kwangbok-dong 2-ga, Chung-gu, ph (051) 241-1051/5 - 84 rooms - restaurant, night club, cocktail bar - W55,000 (US$86).
Crown, 830-30 Pomil 1-dong, Tong-gu, ph (051) 69-1241 - 113 rooms - restaurant, night club, cocktail bar, health club, sauna - $55,000 (US86).
*Kukje*, 830-62 Pomil 2-dong, Tong-gu, ph (051) 744-1331 - 126 rooms - restaurant, night club, cocktail bar, sauna - W52,000 (US$82).
*Nam Tae Pyung Yang* 149-1 Omgung-dong, Puk-gu, ph (051) 328-9911 - 14 rooms - restaurant, theatre restaurant, night club, cocktail bar, sauna - W51,570 (US$81).
*Pusan*, 12.2ga Tonggwang-dong, Chung-gu, ph (051) 241-430-1/9 - 267 rooms - restaurant, night club, cocktail bar, sauna - W50,710 (US$80).
Sapphire, 302-1 Tangni-dong, Saha-gu, ph (051) 207-1300 - 42 rooms - restaurant, night club, cocktail bar, sauna - W50,000 (US$78).
*Phoenix*, 8-1 Namp'o-dong 5-ga, Chung-gu. ph (051) 245-8061/9 - 96 rooms - restaurant, cocktail bar - W42,900 (US$67).
Empire, 398-14 Tokch'on 2-dong, Puk-gu, ph (051) 327-8811 - 40 rooms - restaurant, night club, cocktail bar - W40,250 (US$63).
*Mirabo*, 1124-25 Yonsan-dong, Tongnae-gu, ph (051) 866-7400 - 41 rooms - restaurant, night club, cocktail bar, sauna - W35,000-47,000 (US$55-74).
*Tongnae*, 212 Onch'on-dong, Tongnae-gu, ph (051) 555-1121 - 57 rooms - restaurant, night club, health club, sauna, hot spring bath - W33,000 (US$52).

## Second Class Hotels
*South Palace*, 541-6 Annam-dong, So-gu, ph (051) 254-2000 - 44

rooms - restaurant, cocktail bar - W43,560 (US$68).

*Neul Bom*, 178-7 Pujon 2-dong, Tongnae-gu, ph (051) 555-1800 - 59 rooms - restaurant - W39,900 (US$63).

Haeundae, 524-5 U 1-dong, Haeundae-gu, ph (051) 741-5300 28 rooms - restaurant, cocktail bar - W36,300 (US$57).

*Victoria*, 536-7 Kwaebop-dong, Puk-gu, ph (051) 313-0081 - 38 rooms - restaurant, night club, cocktail bar, sauna - W35,000-36,000 (US$55-56).

*Bando*, 36 Chung-ang-dong 4-ga, Chung-gu, ph (051) 469-0561/7 - 54 rooms - restaurant, cocktail bar - W33,400 (US$52).

*Shin Shin*, 263-11 Pujon 1-dong, Pusanjin-gu, ph (051) 816-0360 - 35 rooms - restaurant, cocktail bar, sauna - W33,000 (US$52).

*Prima*, 739-4 Yonsan 4-dong, Tongnae-gu, ph (051) 867-7500 - 45 rooms - cocktail bar, sauna - W33,000 (US$52).

*Utopia*, 50-3 Kwang-an 3-dong, Nam-gu, ph (051) 757-1100 - 37 rooms - night club, cocktail bar, sauna - W30,000 (US$47).

*Dongil*, 183-9 Onch'on-dong, Tongnae-gu, ph (051) 556-2222 - 34 rooms - restaurant - W29,900-39,000 (US$47-61).

*Dong Bang*, 210-82 Onch'on 1-dong, Tongnae-gu, ph (051) 552-9511/6 - 27 rooms - restaurant, cocktail bar, sauna - W25,300 (US$40).

*Moon Hwa*, 517-65 Pujon 2-dong, Chung-gu, (051) 806-8001/7 - 48 rooms - restaurant, night club, cocktail bar, sauna - W19,960-21,860 (US$31-34).

### Third Class Hotels

*Tower*, 20 Toggwang-dong 3-ga, Chung-gu, (051) 241-5151/9 - 110 rooms - cocktail bar, night club - W34,200 (US$54).

*More*, 226-5 Pujon 2-dong, Pusanjin-gu, ph (051) 803-0070/3 - 18 rooms - restaurant, cocktail bar, sauna - W33,000 (US$52).

*Green Beach*, 1130 Chung 1-dong, Haeundae-gu, ph (051) 742-3211/8 - 46 rooms - restaurant, cocktail bar - W31,900 (US$50).

*Tae Yang*, 1-62 Sujong 2-dong, Tong-gu, ph (051) 465-7311/4 - 59 rooms - restaurant - W29,700 (US$46).

Rio Rio, 1764-7 Taeyon-dong, Nam-gu, ph (051) 642-2525 - 31 rooms - restaurant, cocktail bar - W29,000 (US$45).

*Hillside*, 743-33 Yongu 1-dong, Chung-gu, ph (051) 464-0567/9 - 25 rooms - restaurant - W28,925 (US$45).

Prince, 450-5 Suyong-dong, Nam-gu, ph (051) 755-3333 - 23 rooms - sauna - W28,620 (US$45-58).

*Palace*, 192-18 Kwang-ann, 2-dong, Nam-gu, ph (051) 755-5001/3 - 27 rooms - cocktail bar - W28,480 (US$45).

*Clover*, 477-2 Koejong 3-dong, Saha-gu, ph (051) 205 6611/3 - 30 rooms - restaurant, night club - W28,000 (US$44).

Kwang Jang, 1200-17 Ch'oryang 3-dong, Tong-gu, ph (051) 464-3141/5 - 26 rooms - restaurant, cocktail bar, sauna - W27,500 (US$43).

*Young-Jin*, 88 Namp'o-dong 5-ga, Chung-gu, ph (051) 246-4856/9 - 26 rooms - sauna - W27,500 (US$43).

*New Sungnam*, 2-3 Ch'ungmu-dong, 1-ga, So-gu, ph (051) 243-8051 - 29 rooms - cocktail bar - W27,000 (US$42).

Seaside, 192-5 Kwang-an, 2-dong, Nam-gu, ph (051) 756-0202 - 25 rooms - restaurant, night club - W26,620-30,250 (US$42-47).

*Tae Jong Dae*, 938-17 Tongsam-dong, Yongdo-gu, ph (051) 414-0111/4 - 26 rooms - restaurant - W26,530 (US$42).

*Liberia*, 199-7 Kwang-an 2-dong, Nam-gu, ph (051) 751-3301 - 23 rooms - restaurant - W26,400 (US$41).

*Moon Hwa Oncheon*, 135-4 Onch'on-dong, Tongnae-gu, ph (051) 555-2858 - 16 rooms - cocktail bar, sauna, hot spring bath - W25,419-26,620 (US$40-42).

*Dong Hwa*, 25-6 Namch'on-dong, Nam-gu, ph (051) 626-4001 - 30 rooms - restaurant, sauna - W24,958 (US$39).

Korea, 888-8 Taeyon-dong, Nam-gu, ph (051) 628-7001 - 45 rooms - restaurant, cocktail bar, night club, theatre restaurant - W24,794 (US$39).

*Plaza*, 1213-14 Ch'oryang-dong, Tong-gu, ph (051) 463-5011 /9 - 55 rooms - restaurant, cocktail bar - W24,793 (US$39).

*Korea City*, 830-65 Pomil-dong, Tong-gu, ph (051) 643-7788 - 22 rooms - restaurant - W24,200 (US$38).

*New Life*, 830-172 Pomil 2-dong, Tong-gu, ph (051) 67-3001/8 - 20 rooms - restaurant, sauna - W23,967 (US$38).

*UN*, 335-5 Annam-dong, So-gu, ph (051) 248-5181/5 - 43 rooms - restaurant, night club - W23,637 (US37).

*Kaya*, 520-19 Pujon-dong, Pusanjin-gu, ph (051) 803-2700/5 - 30 rooms - restaurant - W23,000 (US$36).

*Oscar*, 522-40 Pujon 2-dong, Pusanjin-gu, ph (051) 807-3800 - 30 rooms - restaurant, sauna - W21,818 (US$34).

*Sam Hwa*, 81-1 Namp'o-dong, Chung-gu, ph (051) 246-4361/2 - 43 rooms - restaurant, cocktail bar - W21,400-25,680 (US$33-40).

*Mok Hwa*, 830-124 Onch'on-dong, Tong-gu, ph (051) 642-9000 - 21 rooms - restaurant - W20,909-22,727 (US$32-36).

*Dae-A*, 257-3 Pujon-dong, Pusanjin-gu, ph (051) 806-3010 - 57 rooms - restaurant, cocktail bar, night club, sauna - W19,010 (US$30).

# Taegu

### Deluxe Hotels

*Prince*, 1824-2 Taemyong 2-dong, Nam-gu, ph (053) 628-1001 - 76 rooms - restaurant, cocktail bar, health club, night club, sauna - W68,000 (US$107).

*Kumho*, 28 Haso-dong, Chung-gu, ph (053) 252-6001 - 22 rooms - restaurant, cocktail bar, health club, night club, sauna - W66,000 (US$104).

*Grand*, 563-1 Pomo-dong, Susong-gu, ph (053) 742-0001 - 74 rooms - restaurant, cocktail bar, health club, night club, sauna - W66,000 (US$104).

*Park*, San 97-1 Manch'on-dong, Susong-gu, ph (053) 952-0088 - 97 rooms - restaurant, cocktail bar, health club, indoor & outdoor pool, night club, sauna - W66,000 (US$104).

### First Class Hotels

*Dong Taegu*, 326-1 Sinch'on-dong, Tong-gu, ph (053) 756-6601 - 36 rooms - restaurant, cocktail bar, night club, sauna - W51,400 (US$80).

*Garden*, 688-1 Pongdok-dong, Nam-gu, ph (053) 471-9911 - 38 rooms - restaurant, cocktail bar, night club - W49,000 (US$77).

*Taegu*, 245-9 Naedang-dong, So-gu, ph (053) 559-2100 - 46 rooms - restaurant, cocktail bar, night club, sauna - W46,000 (US$72).

*Soo Sung*, 888-2 Tusan-dong, Susong-gu, ph (053) 763-7311 - 50 rooms - restaurant, cocktail bar, night club, sauna, tennis court - W46,000 (US$72).

*Hillside*, 59-1 Yongsu-dong, Tong-gu, ph (053) 951-0801/10 - 27 rooms - restaurant, cocktail bar - W33,000 (US$52).

*Crystal*, 1196-1 Turyu 1-dong, Talso-gu, ph (053) 252-7799 - 46 rooms - restaurant, cocktail bar, night club, sauna - W42,800 (US$67).

*Ariana*, 200-1 Tusan-dong, Susong-gu, ph (053) 765-7776 - 41 rooms - restaurant, cocktail bar, night club - W42,000 (US$66).

*New Young Nam*, 177-7 Pomo-dong, Susong-gu, ph (053) 752-1001/5 - 42 rooms - restaurant, sauna - W40,000-50,000 (US$63-78).

*New Samil,* 200 Songhyon-dong, Talso-gu, ph (053) 629-5501 - 40 rooms - restaurant, cocktail bar, night club, sauna, hot spring bath - W40,000-43,000 (US$63-67).

*Hwang Sil,* 45-1 Shinch'on-dong, 3-ga, Tong-gu, ph (053) 751-2301/4 - 21 rooms - restaurant, cocktail bar, night club. W40,000 (US$63).

*Hwang Kum,* 847-1 Hwanggum-dong, Sunsong-gu, ph (053) 765-6006 - 29 rooms - restaurant, cocktail bar, sauna - W40,000 (US$63).

*Dong In,* 5-2 Samdok-dong 1 ga, Chung-gu, ph (053) 426-5211/9 - 81 rooms - restaurant, cocktail bar, night club - W38,100-53,400 (US$60-84).

### Second Class Hotels

*Ap San,* 1713-2 Taemyong 5-dong, Nam-gu, ph (053) 629-8800 - 36 rooms - restaurant, cocktail bar - W32,700 (US$51).

*Hilltop,* 3048-35 Taemyong, 4-dong, Nam-gu, ph (053) 651-2001 - 36 rooms - restaurant, cocktail bar - W31,405 (US$49).

*Pal Kong,* 90-1 Yongsu-dong, Tong-gu, ph (053) 958-0801/9 - 32 rooms - restaurant, cocktail bar - W29,900 (US$47).

*Arirang,* 474-5 Turyu 3-dong, Talso-gu, ph (053) 624-4000 - 41 rooms - restaurant, cocktail bar - W29,200 (US$46).

*Riverside,* 1006-34 Ipsok-dong, Tong-gu, ph (053) 982-8877 - 34 rooms - restaurant, cocktail bar, night club, sauna - W27,000 (US$42).

*Union,* 1-9 T'aep'yongno, 2-ga, Chung-gu, ph (053) 252-2221 - 36 rooms - restaurant, sauna - W26,115 (US$41).

*Dong San,* 360 Tongsan-dong, Chung-gu, ph (053) 253-7711 - 21 rooms - restaurant, cocktail bar, health club, night club, sauna - W25,620 (US$40).

*Kukje,* 45-1 Kongp'yong-dong, Chung-gu, ph (053) 422-3131/5 - 26 rooms - cocktail bar, sauna - W24,793 (US$39).

### Third Class Hotels

*New Jongro,* 23 Chongno 2-ga, Chung-gu, ph (053) 23-7111/10 - 26 rooms - restaurant, night club - W25,410 (US$41).

*Emerald,* 459-7 Pokhyon-dong, Puk-gu, ph (053) 951-3031 - 27 rooms - restaurant, cocktail bar - W25,200 (US$40).

*Empire,* 63 Pisan-dong, So-Gu, ph (053) 555-3381/4 - 23 rooms - restaurant, night club - W25,000 (US$39).

*Royal,* 24-4 Namil-dong, Chung-gu, ph (053) 253-5546 - 42 rooms - restaurant - W19,600 (US$31).

# Inch'on

### Deluxe Hotels

*Songdo Beach*, 823 Tongch'un-dong, Nam-gu, ph (032) 865-1311/20 -
173 rooms - restaurant, cocktail bar, health club, sauna, hot spring
bath - W57,000 (US$89).

### First Class Hotels

*Galaxy*, 275-1 Kansok-dong, Namdong-gu, ph (032)
421-9111 - 70 rooms - restaurant, cocktail bar, night club, sauna -
W56,000 (US$88).

*Royal*, 173-4 Kansok-dong, Namdong-gu, ph (032) 421-3300 - 43 rooms
- restaurant, cocktail bar, health club, night club, sauna - W55,000
(US$86).

*Olympus*, 3-2 Hang-dong 1-ga, Chung-gu, ph (032) 762-5181
- 171 rooms - restaurant, casino, cocktail bar, night club, sauna -
W51,500 (US$80).

*New Star*, 29 Shinhung-dong, 3-ga, Chung-gu, ph (032)
883-9841/7 - 45 rooms - restaurant, cocktail bar, night club -
W45,000 (US$70).

### Second Class Hotels

*Bu Pyung*, 181 Kalsan-dong, Puk-gu, ph (032) 527-2331/5 - 23 rooms
- restaurant, cocktail bar, sauna - W48,400 (US$76).

*Bosung*, 141-8 Chuan 1-dong, Nam-gu, ph (032) 433-2221/7 - 20
rooms - restaurant, cocktail bar, sauna - W38,000 (US$60).

*Seohae*, 629-7 Yonghyon, 5-dong, Nam-gu, ph (032) 885-9981 - 26
rooms - restaurant, cocktail bar, sauna - W37,190 (US$58).

### Third Class Hotels

*Paegun*, 182-200 Shipchong-dong, Puk-gu, ph (032) 529-4411/8
- 24 rooms - restaurant, cocktail bar, sauna - W35,000 (US$55).

*Soobong* 618-2 Tohwa-dong, Nam-gu, ph (032) 868-6611/5 - 22
rooms - restaurant, cocktail bar, sauna - W30,000 (US$47).

# Taejon

### Deluxe Hotels

*Riviera Yousong*, 444-5 Pongmyong-dong, Yusong-gu, ph
(042)823-2111 - 86 rooms - restaurant, health club, indoor & outdoor

pool, night club, sauna, hot spring bath - W84,000 (US$132).
*Yousoung,* 480 Pongmyong-dong, Yusong-gu, ph (042) 822 2111 -
117 rooms - restaurant, cocktail bar, health club, indoor pool, night
club, hot spring bath - W71,000 (US$111).

### First Class Hotels
*Adria,* 442-5 Pongmyong-dong, Yusong-gu, ph (042)
824-0211 - 40 rooms - restaurant, cocktail bar, sauna - W63,000
(US$99).
*Kuong Won,* 282-27 Yongmun-dong, So-gu, ph (042)
534-8877 - 49 rooms - restaurant, cocktail bar, sauna - W54,450
(US$85).
*Picasso,* 63-31 Yongon-dong, Tong-gu, ph (042) 627-3001/10 - 39 rooms
- restaurant, night club, sauna - W41,000 (US$64).

### Second Class Hotels
*Lucky,* 332-28 Yuch'on-dong, Chung-gu, ph (042) 526-9481
/4 - 20 rooms - restaurant, night club, sauna - W56,000 (US$88).
*Princess,* 536-3 Pongmyong-dong, Yusong-gu, ph (042)
823-9901 - 25 rooms - restaurant, cocktail bar, sauna - W40,000
(US$63).
*Mu Gung Hwa,* 549-1 Pongmyong-dong, Yousong-gu, ph (042)
822-1234 - 24 rooms - restaurant, sauna, tennis court, hot spring
bath - W39,200 (US$62).
*Sae Seoul,* 1-221 Munhwa-dong, Chung-gu, ph (042) 252-8161
- 20 rooms - restaurant, cocktail bar, health club, night club, sauna,
tennis court - W39,000 (US$61).
*Family,* 460-3 Taehung 2-dong, Chung-gu, ph (042) 255
4083/90 - 23 rooms - restaurant, night club - W36,000 (US$56).
*Joongang,* 318 Chung-dong, Tong-gu, ph (042) 253-8801/4 - 38
rooms - night club - W35,100 (US$55).
*Dae Lim,* 230-6 Sonhwa-dong, Chung-gu, ph (042) 255-2161
/7 - 31 rooms - restaurant, cocktail bar - W34,100 (US$53).
*Tae Jeon,* 20-16 Won-dong, Tong-gu, ph (042) 273-8131/9 - 29 rooms
- restaurant, cocktail bar - W33,200 (US$52).
*Life,* 31-50 Chong-dong, Tong-gu, ph (042) 253-5337/40 - 23 rooms -
restaurant, night club, sauna - W31,944 (US$50).
*Prince,* 212-3 Taehung 1-dong, Chung-gu, ph (042)
253-5853/4 - 14 rooms - restaurant, cocktail bar, sauna - W30,000
(US$47).
*Moon Hwa,* 47-55 Chung-dong, Tong-gu, ph (042) 266-7000 - 26
rooms - restaurant, cocktail bar, sauna - W30,000 (US$47).

*Dong-Yang*, 68-20 Yongon-dong, Tong-gu, ph (042) 627-0011/5
- 19 rooms - cocktail bar, night club - W27,600 (US$43).

# Kwangju

### Deluxe Hotels
*Mudungsan*, 9-2 Chisan-dong, Tong-gu, ph (062) 226-0026 - 75
rooms - restaurant, cocktail bar, health club, indoor pool, night
club, sauna, tennis court, hot spring bath - W82,522 (US$129).

### First Class Hotels
*Koreana*, 120-9 Sinan-dong, Puk-gu, ph (062) 526-8600 - 25 rooms -
restaurant, cocktail bar, night club, sauna - W63,500 (US$100).
*City Hill*, 66-8 Unam-dong, Puk-gu, ph (062) 524-0025 - 54 rooms -
restaurant, cocktail bar, night club, sauna - W60,000 (US$94).
*Shin Yank Park*, San 140 Chisan-dong, Tong-gu, ph (062) 228-8000
- 69 rooms - restaurant, cocktail bar, heath club, indoor pool, night
club, sauna - W49,590 (US$78).
Mudung New World, 1003-280 Songjong-dong, Kwangsan-gu, ph
(062) 942-9111 - 44 rooms - restaurant, cocktail bar, night club,
sauna, hot spring bath - W47,934 (US$72).
*Kukje*, 1287-2 Chuwol-dong, So-gu, ph (062) 673-0700 - 35 rooms -
restaurant, cocktail bar, sauna - W46,562 (US$73).
*Palace*, 1154 Hwanggum-dong, Tong-gu, ph (062) 222-2525 - 24
rooms - restaurant, night club, sauna - W44,049 (US$69).
*Grand*, 121 Pullo-dong, Tong-gu, ph (062) 224-6111/5 - 32 rooms -
restaurant, cocktail bar, night club, sauna - W41,404-60,000
(US$65-94).

### Second Class Hotels
*Gran Prix*, 868-4 Hak-dong, Tong-gu, ph (062) 225-7222 - 35 rooms -
restaurant, cocktail bar, sauna - W53,720 (US$84).

# Kyonggi-do

### Deluxe Hotels
*Miranda*, 408-1 Anhung-ri Ich'on-up, Ich'on-gun, ph (0336) 33-2001
- 81 rooms - restaurant, cocktail bar, health club, indoor & outdoor
pools, night club, sauna, hot spring bath - W90,000 (US$141).

### First Class Hotels

*Punchon Grand*, 560 Shimgok-dong, Nam-gu, Puch'on, ph (032) 611-5500 - 38 rooms - restaurant, cocktail bar, night club, sauna - W50,000 (US$78).

*Seoul Hof*, 1-15 Pyollyang-dong, Kwach'on, ph (02) 504-2211 - 47 rooms - restaurant, cocktail bar, health club, sauna - W48,000 (US$75).

*Rasung*, 846-3 Wonkok-dong, Ansan, ph (0345) 80-6161 - 67 rooms - restaurant, cocktail bar, night club, sauna - W39,000 (US$61).

### Second Class Hotels

*Diana*, 447 Ch'olsan-dong, Kwangmyong, ph (02) 616-5161 - 46 rooms - restaurant, cocktail bar, night club - W55,000 (US$86).

*Dong Suwon*, 144-43 Uman-daong, P'alttal-gu, Suwan, ph (0331) 211-6666 - 62 rooms - restaurant, night club, sauna - W46,281 (US$72).

*Seol Bong* 315-5 Anhung-ri, Ich'on-up, Ich'on-gun, ph (0336) 635-5701 - 34 rooms - restaurant, indoor pool, night club, sauna, hot spring bath - W44,497 (US$69).

*Greenpia*, 180-371 Annyong-ri, T'aean-up, Hwassong-gun, ph (0331) 342-3070/8 - 25 rooms - restaurant, cocktail bar. W40,000 (US$62).

*Brown*, 47 Kuch'on-dong, Chang-an-gu, Suwon, ph (0331) 46-4141 /5 - 60 rooms - restaurant, sauna, hot spring bath-W39,050 (US$61).

*Evergreen*, 386-9 Sok'hyon-n, Changhung-myon, Yangju-gun, ph (0351) 45-1170/5 - 22 rooms - restaurant, cocktail bar, night club, sauna - W37,450 (US$58).

*Suk San*, 1-2 Kyo-dong, Kwonson-gu, Suwon, ph (0331) 46-0011 /7 - 24 rooms - restaurant, cocktail bar, sauna - W36,900 (US$58).

Haengju, 331-12 T'odang-dong, Koyang, ph (0344) 974-0011/8 - 43 rooms - restaurant, cocktail bar, night club, sauna - W36,000 (US$56).

Song Tan, 274-190 Shinjang-dong, Songt'an, ph (0333) 666-5101 - 94 rooms - restaurant, night club - W36,000 (US$56-85).

New Korea, 674-251 Anyang 1-dong, Manan-gu, Anyang, ph (0343) 48-6671/80 - 106 rooms - restaurant, night club, sauna - W35,670 (US$56).

*Grand*, 199-3 Uijongbu-dong, Uijongbu, ph (0351) 42-3501 - 29 rooms - restaurant, cockatil bar, night club, sauna - W35,000 (US$55).

*New Prince*, 139-14 Shimgok-dong, Chung-gu, P'och'on-gun, ph (032) 654-3391 - 30 rooms - restaurant, cocktail bar - W35,000 (US$55).

*Sung Nam*, 4002 Sujin-dong, Sujong-gu, Songnam, ph (0342) 752-6200/10 -28 rooms - restaurant, nightclub, sauna - W34,710 (US$54).

*You Lim*, 728-6 Saeng-yon-dong, Tongduch'on, ph (0351) 865-5196 - 43 rooms - restaurant, cocktail bar, night club W32,727 (US$51).

*Kwa Chon*, 1-8 Pyollyang-dong, Kwach'on, ph (02) 504-0071 /7 - 35 rooms - restaurant, cocktail bar, sauna - W30,000 (US$47).

*Youngchon*, 324-14 Shinjang, Song'tan, ph (0333) 63-4000/4 - 52 rooms - restaurant, outdoor pool, night club, sauna, hot spring bath - W28,000 (US$44).

*Pyongtaek*, 62-10 P'yongt'aek-dong, P'yongt'aek, ph (0333) 54-3333 - 37 rooms - Bed only W25,000 (US$39).

### Third Class Hotels

*Koam*, 431-10 Anyang 6-dong, Anyang, ph (0343) 45-6601 - 27 rooms - Bed only W30,000 (US$47).

*Sala Park*, 548-10 Saengyon-dong, Tong-duch'on, ph (0351) 62-7171 - 34 rooms - restaurant, cocktail bar, sauna - W23,000 (US$36).

*Kang Won Garden*, 291 P'yongt'aek-dong, P'yongt'aek, ph (0333) 52-2020/3 - 32 rooms - restaurant, cocktail bar. W21,300-24,200 (US$33-38).

# Kangwon-do

### Deluxe Hotels

*Yong Pyeong Dragon Valley*, 130 Yongsan-ri, Toam-myon, Pyongch'ang-gun, ph (0374) 32-5757 - 30 rooms - restaurant, cocktail bar, health club, indoor pool, night club, sauna, tennis court - W78,500 (US$123).

### First Class Hotels

*New Sorak*, 106-1 Sorak-dong, Sokch'o, ph (0392) 34-7131/49 - 78 rooms - restaurant, cocktail bar, night club - W61,000 (US$95).

*Rio*, 300-3 Samchong-dong, Ch'unch'on, ph (0392) 56-2525 - 60 rooms - restaurant, cocktail bar, night club, sauna - W55,000 (US$86).

*Nak San Beach*, 3-2 Chonjin-ri, Kanghyon-myon, Yangyang -gun, ph (0396) 672-4000 - 53 rooms - restaurant, cocktail bar, night club, hot spring bath - W51,000 (US$80).

*Kangnung,* 1117 P'onam-dong, Kangnung, ph (0391) 41-3771 - 38 rooms - restaurant, cocktail bar, sauna - W50,000-60,000 (US$78-94).
*Hong Chon,* 62-11 Chin-ri, Hongch'on-up, Hongch'on-gun, ph (0366) 33-9111/9 - 28 rooms - restaurant, cocktail bar, night club, sauna - W45,980 (US$72).
*Chuncheon Sejong,* San 1 Pong-ui-dong, Ch'unch'on, (0361) 52-1191/6 - 43 rooms - restaurant, cocktail bar, outside pool - W45,000 (US$70).

## Second Class Hotels
*Sokcho Beach,* 748-19 Chung-ang-dong, Sokch'o, ph (0392) 31-8700 - 30 rooms - restaurant, cocktail bar, night club   - W49,755-68,000 (US$78-106).
*Dong Hae,* 274-1 Kangmun-dong, Kargnung, ph (0391) 44-2181 /5 - 50 rooms - restaurant, indoor pool, tennis court - W48,000 (US$75).
*Kyungpo Beach,* 303-4 Kangmun-dong, Kangnung, ph (0391) 44-2277/9 - 40 rooms - restaurant, cocktail bar, W42,000 (US$66).
*New Dong Hae,* 484 Ch'ongok-dong, Tonghae, ph (0394) 33-9215 - 30 rooms - restaurant, cocktail bar, night club, sauna - W42,000 (US$66).
*Chun Chon,* 30-1 Nagwon-dong, Ch'urch'on, ph (0361) 55-3300/3 - 32 rooms - restaurant, cocktail bar, night club - W36,300 (US$57).
*Won Ju,* 63-1 Chung-ang-dong, Wonju, ph (0371) 43-1241/50 - 45 rooms - restaurant, cocktail bar, night club, sauna - W35,000 (US$55).

## Third Class Hotels
Soraksan, 151 Sorak-dong, Sokch'o, ph (0392) 34-710/5 - 24 rooms - cocktail bar - W40,000 (US$62).
*Sambuyeon,* 626 Shinch'olwon-ri, Kalmal-up, Ch'olwon-gun, ph (0353) 52-5884 - 15 rooms - restaurant - W40,000 (US$62).
*Koreana,* 257-6 Kangmun-dong, Kangnung, ph (0391) 44-2701/6 - 30 rooms - Bed only W38,800 (US$61).
*Taebaek,* 25-6 Hwangji-dong, T'aebaek, ph (0395) 52-7711 - 30 rooms - restaurant, cocktail bar, night club, sauna - W36,300 (US$57).
*Imperial,* San 84-2 Chumunjin, Chumunjin-up, Myongju-gun, ph (0391) 661-1953 - 28 rooms - restaurant, outdoor pool, tennis court - W36,000 (US$56).
*Royal,* 395-12 Upsang-ri, Hiengsong-up, Hoengsong-gun, ph (0372) 42-6601 - 35 rooms - restaurant, cocktail bar, health club, indoor pool, night club, sauna - W35,000 (US$55).

# Ch'ungch'ongbuk-do

### First Class Hotels

*Suanbo Sang Nok*, 292 Onch'on-ri, Sangmo-myon, Chung-won-gun, ph (0441) 845-3500 - 32 rooms - restaurant, cocktail bar, night club, sauna, hot springs bath - W50,800 (US$79).

*Songnisan*, 198 Sanae-ri, Naesongni-myon, Poun-gun, ph (0433) 42-5281/8 - 34 rooms - restaurant, casino, cocktil bar, outdoor pool, tennis - W50,000 (US$78).

*Chungju*, 855 Pongbang-dong, Ch'ungju, ph (0441) 43-8181/5 - 32 rooms - restaurant, cocktail bar, health club, indoor pool, night club, sauna - W48,100 (US$75).

*Kukje*, 35-7 Piha-dong, Ch'ongju, ph (0431) 67-5522 - 47 rooms - restaurant, cocktail bar, night club, sauna - W48,100 (US$75).

*Waikiki Suanbo*, 806-1 Onch'on-ri, Sangmo-myon, Chung-won-gun, ph (0441) 846-3333 - 26 rooms - restaurant, cocktail bar, indoor pool, night club, sauna, hot springs bath - W47,400 (US$74).

Chungju Imperial, 102-1 Hoam-dong, Ch'ungju, ph (0441) 848-0470/9 - 24 rooms - restaurant, cocktail bar, health club, night club, sauna - W47,000 (US$74).

*Ch'ungjuho Resort*, 472 Hach'on-ri, Tongyang-myon, Chungwon-gun, ph (0441) 851-2800/2 - 40 rooms - restaurant, cocktail bar, indoor pool, outdoor pool, sauna, tennis court - W46,000 (US$72).

*Suanbo Park*, 838-1 Onch'on-ri, Sangmo-myon, Chung-won-gun, ph (0441) 846-2331/6 - 22 rooms - restaurant, health club, indoor pool, night club, sauna, tennis court, hot spring bath - W46,000 (US$72).

Ch'ongju Myongam Park, 2-1 Myongnam-dong, Ch'ongju, ph (0431) 57-7451/6 - 32 rooms - restaurant, cocktail bar, night club - W46,000 (US$72).

*Chungpyeong*, 45-4 Chojung-ri, Chungp'yong-up, Koesan-gun, ph (0441) 36-9889 - 53 rooms - restaurant, cocktail bar, night club - W44,000 (US$69).

### Second Class Hotels

*Sooanbo*, 250 Onch'on-ri, Sangmo-myon, Chung-won-gun, ph (0441) 846-2311/6 - 12 rooms - restaurant, sauna - W39,800 (US$62).

*Chongju*, 844-3 Poktae-dong, Ch'ongju, ph (0431) 64-2181/3 - 53 rooms

- restaurant, cocktail bar, night club - W38,200 (US$60).
*Chong Ju Royal*, 227-21 Somun-dong, Ch'ongju, ph (0431) 221-1300 - 21 rooms - restaurant, cocktail bar, health club, night club, sauna - W38,000 (US$60).
*Chungju Pastel*, 269 Yokjon-dong, Ch'ungju, ph(0441) 848-1185 - 29 rooms - restaurant, cocktail bar, sauna - W35,000 (US$55).

### Third Class Hotels

*Jinyang*, 1831 Pongmyong-dong, Ch'ongju, ph (0431) 67-1121/5 - 32 rooms - restaurant - W38,500 (US$60).
*Danyang Park*, 93 T'obang-ri, Tanyang-up, Tanyang-gun, ph (0444) 22-6000/2 - 7 rooms - restaurant - W34,848 (US$55).
*Eum Sung*, 1360-1 Yongsan-ri, Umsong-up, Umsong-gun, ph (0446) 72-1961 - 21 rooms - restaurant - W33,880 (US$53).
*Chechon*, 11-1 Myong-dong, Chech'on, ph (0443) 43-4111/4 - 12 rooms - restaurant, sauna - W27,300 (US$43).
*Dae Ho*, 174-9 Kumgu-ri, Okch'on-up, Okch'on-gun, ph (0475) 32-0001 - 9 rooms - sauna. W25,000-30,000- US$39-47.
*Jin Cheon*, 240-1 Umnae-ri, Chinch'on-up, Chinch'on-gun, ph (0434) 33-0012 - 17 rooms -restaurant, night club, sauna - W25,000 (US$39).

# Ch'ungch'ongnam-do

### First Class Hotels

*Dogo Royal*, 174-13 Kigok-ri, Togo-myon, Asan-gun, ph (0418) 43-5511/20 - 23 rooms - restaurant, cocktail bar, indoor pool, night club, sauna, hot springs bath - W62,000 (US$97).
*Onyang*, 242-10 Onch'on-dong, Onyang, ph (0481) 545-2141 - 32 rooms - restaurant, cocktail bar, heath club, indoor pool, night club, sauna - W55,000-75,000 (US$86-117).
Onyang Grand Park, 300-28 Onch'on-dong, Onyang, ph (0418) 43-9711 - 60 rooms - restaurant, cocktail bar, night club, sauna - W54,600 (US$85).
*Jeil*, 228-6 Onch'on-dong, Onyang, ph (0418) 44-6111/25 - 70 rooms - restaurant, night club, sauna, hot springs bath - W53,000 (US$83).
*Paradise Dogo*, 180-1 Kigok-ri, Togo-myon, Asan-gun, ph (0418) 42-6031/9 - 87 rooms - restaurant, cocktail bar, outdoor pool, night club, sauna, tennis court, hot springs bath - W51,770 (US$81).
*New Korea*, 66-1 Panwol-ri, Nonsan-up, Nonsan-gun, ph (0418) 33-4710 - 38 rooms - restaurant, cocktail bar, night club, sauna - W32,000 (US$50).

### Second Class Hotels

*New Gaya*, 163-1 Shinp'yong-ri, Toksan-myon, Yesan-gun, ph (0458) 37-0101/8 - 8 rooms - restaurant, night club, hot springs bath - W40,000-70,000 (US$63-109).

*Westin*, 230-6 Onch'on-dong, Onyang, ph (0418) 42-8151/5 - 37 rooms - restaurant, cocktail bar, sauna, hot spring bath - W34,500 (US$54).

*Konju*, 139-1 Sansong-dong, Kongju, ph (0416) 55-4023/8 - 15 rooms - restaurant, sauna - W33,000 (US$52).

### Third Class Hotels

*Riverside*, 464-5 Shinkwan-dong, Jongju, ph (0416) 55-1001/8 - 34 rooms - restaurant, sauna - W50,000 (US$78).

# Chollabuk-do

### Deluxe Hotels

Core, 627-1 So-nosong-dong, Tokchin-gu, Chonju, ph  (0652) 85-1100 - 54 rooms - restaurant, cocktail bar, night club, sauna - W72,500 (US$114).

### First Class Hotels

*Nae Jang San*, 71-14 Naejang-dong, Chongju, ph (0681) 535-4131/7 - 46 rooms - restaurant, cocktail bar, night club, sauna, tennis court - W58,500 (US$92).

Chonju, 28 Taga-dong 3-ga, Wansan-gu, Chonju, ph (0652) 83-2811/5 - 33 rooms - restaurant, cocktail bar, night club - W35,000-40,000 (US$55-62).

### Third Class Hotels

*Hanovar*, 54-7 Chubg-ang-dong, Iri, ph (0653) 856-0402/5 - 21 rooms - restaurant - W40,000 (US$62).

*Victory*, 21-1 Shinch'ang-dong, Kunsan, ph (0654) 445-6161/3 - 59 rooms - restaurant, night club - W21,780 (US$34).

# Chollanam-do

### First Class Hotels

*Chirisan Plaza*, San 32-1 Hwangjon-ri, Masan-myon, Kurye-gun, ph (0664) 782-2171 - 19 rooms - restaurant, cocktail bar, sauna - W53,500 (US$84).

Chowon, 1-9 Taeui-dong 2-ga, Mokp'o, ph (0631) 43-0055 - 23 rooms - restaurant, cocktail bar, night club, sauna - W50,000 (US$78).

*Shinan Beach*, 440-4 Chukkyo-dong, Mokp'o, ph (0631) 43-3399 - 82 rooms - restaurant, cocktail bar, outdoor pool, night club, sauna - W47,250 (US$74).

Yosu Beach, 346 Ch'ungmu-dong, Yosu, ph (0632) 63-2011/5 - 44 rooms-restaurant, cocktail bar, night club, sauna - W41,818 (US$66).

### Second Class Hotels

Baek Yang, 333-3 Yaksu-ri, Pukha-myon, Changsong-gun, ph (0685) 92-0651 - 18 rooms - restaurant, cocktail bar, night club - W55,000 (US$86).

*Sunchon Royal*, 32-8 Changch'on-dong, Sunch'on, ph (0661) 741-7000 - 39 rooms - restaurant, cocktail bar, sauna - W42,975 (US$67).

*Torim World*, San 15 Wolbong-ri, Koksong-up, Koksong-gun, ph (0688) 62-9111/14 - 25 rooms - Bed only W42,149 (US$66).

*Keumgang*, 22-20 Namnae-dong, Sunch'on, ph (0661) 52-8301/7 - 48 rooms - restaurant, cocktail bar, night club, sauna - W40,000-43,000 (US$63-67).

Yosu Sejong, 1054-1 Konghwa-dong, Yosu, ph (0662) 62-6111 - 20 rooms - restaurant, cocktail bar, sauna - W31,400 (US$49).

*Garden*, 1247 Kunnae-ri, Wando-up, Wando-gun, ph (0633) 52-5001 - 10 rooms - restaurant, cocktail bar, night club - W30,250 (US$47).

Daihwa, 77-9n Hak-dong, Yoch'on, ph (0622) 83-4661/5 - 27 rooms - restaurant, cocktail bar, sauna - W29,958 (US$47).

*Yosu Park*, 979-1 Kwanmun-dong, Yosu, ph (0662) 63-2335/8 - 14 rooms - restaurant, cocktail bar, night club, sauna - W19,800 (US$31).

### Third Class Hotels

*Yosu*, 766 Konghwa-dong, Yosu, ph (0662) 62-3131/5 - 26 rooms - restaurant, cocktail bar, night club - W30,000-38,000 (US$47-60).

# Kyongsangbuk-do

### Super Deluxe Hotels

*Kyongju Hilton*, 370 Shinp'yong-dong, Kyongju, ph (0561) 745-7788 -

311 rooms - restaurant, cocktail bar, health club, indoor & outdoor pools, night club, sauna, hot springs bath - W110,000-118,000 (US$173-185).

*Concorde*, 410 Shinp'yong-dong, Kyongju, ph (0561) 745-7000 - 292 rooms - restaurant, cocktail bar, outdoor pool, sauna, hot springs bath - W110,000 (US$173).

Kyong Ju Chosun, 410 Shinp'yong-dong, Kyongju, ph (0561) 745-7701/9 - 262 rooms - restaurant, cocktail bar, indoor & outdoor pools, night club, sauna, tennis court, hot springs bath - W104,060-121,000 (US$163-190).

*Hyundae*, 477-2 Shinp'yong-dong, Kyongju, ph (0561) 748-2233 - 413 rooms - restaurant, health club, indoor & outdoor pool, sauna, tennis court, hot spring bath - W95,000 (US$149).

*Kolon*, 111-1 Ma-dong, Kyongju, ph (0561) 746-9001/11 - 284 rooms - restaurant, casino, cocktail bar, outdoor pool, night club, sauna, tennis court, hot springs bath - W92,000-120,000 (US$144-188).

## Deluxe Hotels

*Cignus*, 145-21 Yonghung-dong, P'ohang, ph (0562) 75-2000 - 96 rooms - restaurant, cocktail bar, health club, night club, sauna, hot springs bath - W80,000 (US$125).

## First Class Hotels

*Kyongju Spa*, 145-1 Kujong-dong, Kyongju, ph (0561) 746-6661/4 - 23 rooms - restaurant, cocktail bar, night club, sauna -- W63,525 (US$100).

Paekam Tonghae, 144-2 Sot'ae-ri, Onjong-myon, Ulchin-gum, ph (0565) 787-3801/9 - 28 rooms - restaurant, cocktail bar, indoor pool, night club, sauna, hot springs bath - W55,000 (US$86).

*Kimchon Grand*, 575 Pugok-dong, Kimch'on, ph (0547) 33-9001 - 38 rooms - restaurant, cocktail bar, heath club, night club, sauna - W50,000 (US$78).

Baekam Resort, 964 Onjong-ri, Onjong-myon, Ulchin-gun, ph (0565) 787-3500 - 44 rooms - restaurant, cocktail bar, health spa, outdoor pool, night club, sauna, hot springs bath - W48,000 (US$75).

*Kumi*, 1032-5 Wonp'yong-dong, Kumi, ph (0546) 51-2001/8 - 42 rooms - restaurant, cocktail bar, sauna - W45,000 (US$70).

*Ocean Park*, 614-6 Chukto 2-dong, P'ohang, ph (0562) 77-5555 - 42 rooms - restaurant, cocktail bar, night club, sauna - W40,300 (US$63).

*Andong Park*, 324 Unhung-dong, Andong, ph (0571) 57-5445 - 35 rooms

- restaurant, cocktail bar - W40,000 (US$63).
*Sae Jae*, 159-4 Chomch'on-dong, Chomch'on, ph (0581) 53-8000
- 43 rooms - restaurant, cocktail bar, health club, night club -
W37,190 (US$58).
*Sobaeksan*, 531-1 Kahung-dong, Yongju, ph (0572) 34-3300/5 - 28 rooms
- restaurant, cocktail bar, health club, sauna, tennis court - W35,000
(US$55).

### Second Class Hotels
*Kumi Prince*, 205 Kongdan-dong, Kumi, ph (0546)
461-8981/7 - 31 rooms - restaurant, cocktail bar, sauna - W46,000
(US$72).
*Kyongju*, 645 Shinp'yong-dong, Kyongju, ph (0561) 745-7123 - 32
rooms - restaurant, cocktail bar - W36,000 (US$56).
*Hwang Shill*, 152-9 Noso-dong, Kyongju, ph (0561) 745-3500 - 18 rooms
- cocktail bar, health club, sauna - W36,000 (US$56).
Mandarin, 49-18 Chukto-dong, P'ohang, ph (0562) 73-6666 - 25
rooms - restaurant, cocktail bar, sauna - W34,500 (US$54).
*Olympus*, 438-1 Songdo-dong, P'ohang, ph (0562) 41-6001 - 53
rooms - restaurant, cocktail bar, sauna - W33,000 (US$51).
*Sung Ryu Park*, 968-5 Onjong-ri, Onjong-myon, Ulchin-gum, ph
(0565) 787-3711/5 - 19 rooms - restaurant, cocktail bar, night club,
tennis court, hot springs bath - W32,100 (US$50).
*Pohang Beach*, 311-2 Songdo-dong, P'ohang, ph (0562)
41-1401/7 - 34 rooms - restaurant, cocktail bar, night club -
W30,250 (US$47).
*Kimchon*, 140-1 Moam-dong, Kimch'on, ph (0547) 32-9911/6 - 27 rooms
- restaurant, cocktail bar, night club, sauna - W30,000 (US$47).
*Sun Prince*, 17 Chung-ang-dong, P'ohang, ph (0562) 42-2800 - 14 rooms
- restaurant, cocktail bar, night club, sauna - W26,000 (US$41).

### Third Class Hotels
Ulung Marina, San 3-4 Sadong-ri, Ulung-up, Ulung-gun, ph (0566)
791-0020 - 6 rooms - restaurant, cocktail bar, night club, tennis
court, hot springs bath - W38,000 (US$60).
*Keumosan*, San 24-6 Namt'ong-dong, Kumi, ph (0546)
52-3151/9 - 107 rooms - restaurant, cocktail bar - W36,300 (US$57).
*Palace*, 144-12 Tongbin-dong 2-ga, P'ohang, ph (0562)
42-4242 - 17 rooms - restaurant, cocktail bar - W32,670 (US$51).
*Ariana*, 130-30 Wonp'yong-dong, Kumi, ph (0562) 51-3700
/7 -33 rooms - cocktail bar, night club, sauna - W32,100 (US$50).

*Juwangsan*, 69-2 Wolmak-ri, Ch'ongsong-up, Ch'ongsong-gun, ph (0575) 72-6801/5 - 22 rooms - restaurant, night club - W24,794 (US$39).

*Donghae Beach*, 68-1 Namho-ri, Namjong-myon, Yongdok -gun, ph (0564) 33-6611 - 15 rooms - restaurant, night club - W25,000 (US$39).

*Sang Dae Hot Spring*, 590 Sangdae-dong, Namsan-myon, Kyongsan-gun, ph (053) 82-8001/2 - 13 rooms - restaurant, sauna - W24,000-28,000 (US$38-44).

*New Riverside*, 315 Pyolam-ri, Hogye-myon, Mun-gyong-gun, ph (0581) 53-4001/3 - 25 rooms - restaurant, cocktail bar, indoor pool, night club, sauna - W22,000 (US$35).

*Kyongju Park*, 170-1 Noso-dong, Kyongju, ph (0561) 42-8804 - 16 rooms - restaurant, night club - W22,066 (US$35).

*Hyup Sung*, 130-6 Noso-dong, Kyongju, ph (0561) 41-3335/9 - 19 rooms - restaurant, cocktail bar, night club, sauna - W20,000 (US$31).

# Kyongsangnam-do

### Deluxe Hotels
*Diamond*, 283 Chonha-dong, Tong-gu, Ulsan, ph (0522) 32-7171 - 276 rooms - restaurant, indoor pool, health club, sauna - W75,000-85,000 (US$118-133).

Koreana, 255-3 Songnam-dong, Chung-gu, Ulsan, ph (0522) 44-9911/20 - 148 rooms - restaurant, cocktail bar, night club, sauna - W65,000 (US$102).

### First Class Hotels
*Bugok*, 326-1 Komun-ri, Pugok-myon, Ch'angnyong-gun, ph (0559) 36-5181/90 - 62 rooms - restaurant, cocktail bar, outdoor pool, night club, suna, hot springs bath - W55,120 (US$86).

*Haeinsa*, 1230-112 Ch'in-ri, Kaya-myon, Hapch'on-gun, ph (0599) 33-2000 - 33 rooms - restaurant, cocktail bar, night club, sauna - W55,000 (US$86).

*Bu Gok Hawii*, 195-7 Komun-ri, Pugok-myon, Ch'angnyong-gun, ph (0559) 36-6331/9 - 42 rooms - restaurant, cocktail bar, health club, outdoor pool, night club, sauna, tennis court. W51,430 (US$81).

*Kimhae*, 827-4 Puwon-dong, Kimhae, ph (0525) 35-0101 - 35 rooms - restaurant, cocktail bar, health club, night club, sauna - W48,000 (US$75).

*Bugok Royal*, 215-1 Komun-ri, Pugok-myon, Ch'angnyong-gun, ph (0559) 36-6661/9 - 75 rooms - restaurant, night club, sauna - W46,000 (US$72).

*Changwon Kukje*, 97-4 Chung-ang-dong, Ch'angwon, ph (0551) 81-1001/9 - 64 rooms - restaurant, night club, sauna - W44,100 (US$69).

*Changwon*, 99-4 Chung-ang-dong, Ch'angwon, ph (0551) 83-55551/60 - 130 rooms - restaurant, cocktail bar, indoor pool, night club, sauna. W42,000 (US$65).

*Lotte Crystal*, 306 Changgun-dong 4-ga, Masan, ph (0551) 45-1112 - 93 rooms - restaurant, cocktail bar, health club, night club, sauna - W41,250-47,300 (US$64-74).

Masan Royal, 215 Sangnam-dong, Masan, ph (0551) 44-1150 - 36 rooms - restaurant, cocktail bar, night club, sauna - W40,700 (US$64).

*Savoy*, 8-2 Sanho-dong, Happ'o-gu, Masan, ph (0551) 47-1011/22 - 53 rooms - restaurant, cocktail bar, night club, sauna - W40,000-45,000 (US$63-70).

*Dongbang*, 803-4 Okpongnam-dong, Chinju, ph (0591) 43-0131/9 - 36 rooms - restaurant, cocktail bar, health club, night club, sauna - W38,000 (US$60).

### Second Class Hotels

Tongdosa, 322-13 Ch'osan-ri, Habuk-myon, Yangsan-gun, ph (0523) 82-7117 - 27 rooms - restaurant, cocktail bar - W50,000 (US$78).

*Crown*, San 10, Sach'ang-ri, Pugok-myon, ph (0559) 36 6263 - 23 rooms - restaurant, cocktail bar, night club, sauna, tennis court - W43,800 (US$68).

*Ulsan*, 570-1 Yaum-dong, Nam-gu, Ulsan, ph (0522) 71-7001/9 - 37 rooms - restaurant, cocktail bar, night club, sauna - W38,060 (US$60).

*Bugok Garden*, 221-1 Komun-ri, Pugok-myon, Ch'angnyong-gun, ph (0559) 36-5771/9 - 28 rooms - restaurant, night club, sauna, hot springs bath - W37,950 (US$60).

*Olympic*, 97-1 Chung-ang-dong, Ch'angwon, ph (0521) 85 3331/4 - 75 rooms - restaurant, cocktail bar, health club, night club, sauna - W37,510 (US$59).

*New Sam Hwa*, 58-5 Polri-dong, Samch'onp'o, ph (0593) 32-9711/7 - 14 rooms - restaurant, cocktail bar, night club, tennis court - W35,000 (US$55).

*Masan Arirang*, 229-17 Sokch'on-dong, Masan, ph (0551) 94-2211 - 36 rooms - restaurant, cocktail bar, night club, sauna. W33,000 (US$52).

*Samcheonpo Beach*, 598-1 Taebang-dong, Samch'onp'o, ph (0593) 32-9801/5 - 19 rooms - restaurant, cocktail bar, night club, sauna - W32,670 (US$51).

*Okpo*, 330-4 Okp'o 1-dong, Chang-sungp'o, ph (0558) 687-3761/5 - 117 rooms - restaurant, cocktail bar, night club, tennis court - W32,500 (US$51).

*Tae Hwa*, 1406-6 Shinjong-dong, Nam-gu, Ulsan, ph (0522) 73-3301/4 - 98 rooms - restaurant, cocktail bar, night club, sauna - W31,030-34,240 (US$49-54).

*Riverside*, 121-2 T'aehwa-dong, Chung-gu, Ulsan, ph (0522) 45-8061 - 30 rooms - cocktail bar, night club, sauna - W31,030 (US$49).

### Third Class Hotels

*New Port*, 1141 Chongyang-dong, Ch'ungmu, ph (0557) 44-4411 - 26 rooms - restaurant, cocktail bar, night club, sauna - W45,000(US$71).

*Bugok Park*, 216-16 Komun-ri, Pugok-myon, Ch'angnyong-gun, ph (0559) 36 6311/6 - 15 rooms - restaurant, cocktail bar, hot springs bath - W38,000 (US$60).

*Chungmu Hallyo*, 156-10 Pongp'yong-dong, Ch'ungmu, ph(0557) 44-9501/8 - 27 rooms -restaurant, cocktail bar, sauna-W33,000 (US$52).

*Joong Ang*, 219-2 Okkyo-dong, Ch'ung-gu, Ulsan, ph (0522) 45-3770 /8 - 26 rooms - restaurant, cocktail bar, sauna - W28,200 (US$44).

# Cheju-do

### Super Deluxe Hotels

*Shilla*, 3039-3 Saektal-dong, Sogwip'o, ph (064) 30-5114 - 272 rooms - restaurant, casino, cocktail bar, health club, indoor & outdoor pools, night club, sauna, tennis court - W140,000-165,000 (US$220-259).

*Hyatt Regency*, 3039-1 Saektal-dong, Sogwip'o, ph (064) 33-1234/40 - 188 rooms - restaurant, casino, cocktail bar, health club, indoor & outdoor pools, night club, sauna, tennis court - W124,000-142,000 (US$195-223).

*Cheju Grand*, 263-15 Yon-dong, Cheju, ph (064) 47-5000 - 507 rooms - restaurant, casino, cocktail bar, outdoor pool, night club, sauna - W77,000-140,000 (US$121-220).

## Deluxe Hotels

*Cheju Nam Seoul*, 291-30 Yen-dong, Cheju, ph (064) 42-4111 - 147 rooms - restaurant, casino, cockail bar, health club, indoor pool, night club, sauna, hot springs bath - W110,000 (US$173).

*Prince*, 731-3 Sohong-dong, Sogwip'o, ph (064) 32-9911/30 - 140 rooms - restaurant, cocktail bar, indoor & outdoor pool, night club, sauna - W70,000-110,000 (US$110-172).

*Cheju KAL*, 1691-9 Ido 1-dong, Cheju, ph (064) 53-6151 - 277 rooms - restaurant, casino, cocktail bar, health club, indoor pool, night club, sauna, hot springs bath - W70,000 (US$110).

*Lagonda*, 159-1 Yongdam 1-dong, Cheju, ph (064) 58-2500 - 133 rooms - restaurant, cocktail bar, sauna - W70,000 (US$110).

*Seogwipo KAL*, 486-3 T'opyong-dong, Sogwip'o, ph (064) 32-9851 - 194 rooms - restaurant, casino, cocktail bar, indoor & outdoor pools, night club, sauna, tennis court - W70,000 (US$110).

*Oriental*, 1197 Samdo 2-dong, Cheju, ph (064) 52-8222 - 185 rooms - restaurant, casino, cocktail bar, sauna - W70,000 (US$110).

## First Class Hotels

*Cheju Royal*, 272-34 Yon-dong, Cheju, ph (064) 43-2222 - 93 rooms - restaurant, cocktail bar, night club, sauna - W67,760 (US$106).

*Paradise Sogwipo* 511 T'op'yong-dong, Sogwip'o, ph (064) 33-5161 - 58 rooms - restaurant, cocktail bar, health club, outdoor pool, sauna - W59,500-140,000 (US$93-219).

Cheju Honey, 1315 Ido 1-dong, Cheju, ph (064) 58-4200 - 46 rooms - restaurant, cocktail bar - W59,500 (US$93).

*Island*, 263-12 Yon-dong, Cheju, (064) 43-0300 - 69 rooms - restaurant, cocktail bar, sauna - W59,500 (US$93).

*Country*, 291-41 Yon-dong, Cheju, ph (064) 47-4900 - 60 rooms - restaurant, cocktail bar, sauna - W59,500 (US$93).

*Sun Beach*, 820-1 Sogwi-dong, Sogwip'o, ph (064) 63-3600 - 54 rooms - restaurant - W59,500 (US$93).

*Cheju Pearl*, 277-2 Yon-dong, Cheju, ph (064) 42-8871 - 60 rooms - restaurant, cocktail bar - W59,500 (US$93).

*Green*, 274-37 Yon-dong, Cheju, ph (064) 42-0071 - 66 rooms - restaurant, health club, night club, sauna - W59,500 (US$93).

*Cheju Seoul*, 1192-20 Samdo 2-dong, Cheju, ph (064) 52-2211 - 89 rooms - restaurant, cocktail bar, night club - W59,500 (US$93).

*Mosu*, 274-13 Yon-dong, Cheju, ph (064) 42-1001 - 104 rooms - restaurant, cocktail bar, night club, sauna - W50,500 (US$79).

*Palace*, 1192-18 Samdo 2-dong, Cheju, ph (064) 53-8811 - 86 rooms -

restaurant, cocktail bar, sauna - W59,500 (US$79).

*Holiday Cheju*, 863 Kosong-ri, Aewol-up, Pukcheju-gun, ph (064) 99-3111 - 92 rooms - restaurant, cocktail bar, night club, sauna - W59,500 (US$79).

### Second Class Hotels

*Hawaii* 278-2 Yon-dong, Cheju, ph (064) 42-0061/63 - 71 rooms - restaurant, cocktail bar - W49,000 (US$77).

*Grace*, 261-23 Yon-dong, Cheju, ph (064) 42-0066 - 49 rooms - restaurant, cocktail bar, sauna - W49,000 (US$77).

*Raja*, 268-10 Yon-dong, Cheju , ph (064) 47-4030/9 - 31 rooms - restaurant, cocktail bar - W49,000 (US$77).

*Tamra*, 272-29 Yon-dong, Cheju, ph (064) 42-0058 - 57 rooms - restaurant, cocktail bar - W49,000 (US$77).

*Cheju Milano*, 273-43 Yon-dong, Cheju, ph (064) 42-0088 - 50 rooms - restaurant - W49,000 (US$77).

*Continental*, 268 Yon-dong, Cheju, ph (064) 47-3390 - 39 rooms - restaurant, cocktail bar - W49,000 (US$77).

*Simong*, 260-9 Yon-dong, Cheju, ph (064) 47-7775 - 44 rooms - restaurant - W46,000 (US$72).

*Marina*, 300-8 Yon-dong, Cheju, ph (064) 46-6161 - 55 rooms - restaurant, cocktail bar - W46,000 (US$72).

### Third Class Hotels

*Sogwipo Park*, 674-1 Sogwi-dong, Sogwip'o, ph (064) 62-2161/7 -34 rooms-restaurant, cocktail bar, night club, sauna-W41,500 (US$65).

*Seaside*, 1192-21 Samdo 2-dong, Cheju, ph (064) 52-0091/8 - 26 rooms - Bed only W41,500 (US$65).

*Seogwipo Lions*, 803 Sogwi-dong, Sogwip'o, ph (064) 62-4141/4 - 39 rooms - night club - W41,500 (US$65).

*VIP Park*, 917-2 Nohyong-dong, Cheju, (064) 43-5530 - 24 rooms - Bed only W41,500 (US$65).

# Youth Hostels

At present there are about eleven Youth Hostels throughout Korea. They are registered with the Korea Youth Hostel Association, and offer reasonably priced rooms for the economy-minded traveller or student. The charges are about US$50 a night for twin share, US$10 per person for dormitory accommodation. Fees are slightly higher in Seoul. For reservations and information ring (02) 725-3031 or call at room 409 Jokson Hyundai Building, 80 Jokson-dong, Chongno-gu, Seoul.

*Olympic Park*, 88 Pang-dong  Songp'a-gu, Seoul, ph (02) 410-2114.

*Dongsong*, 206-11 Songdong-dong, Pusan, ph (051) 743-8466.

*Goyang*, 278 Koyang-dong, Koyang-shi, Kyonggi-do, ph (0344) 62-9049.

*Bulam*, 99 Hwajop'ri, Byolrae-myon, Kyonggi-do, ph (0344) 65-8081.

*Daesungri*, 633-3 Daesong-ri, Oeso-myon, Kap'yong-gun, Kyonggi-do, ph (0356) 84-0144.

*Naksan*, 30-1 Chonjin-ri, Kanghyon-myon, Yangyang-gun, Kangwon-do, ph (0396) 672-3416.

*Yongpyeong*, 130 Yongsan-ri, Doam-myon, P'yongch'ang-gun Kangwon-do, ph (0374) 32-5757.

*Kangchon*, San 98-1 Kangch'on-ri, Namsan-myon, Ch'unch'on-gun, Kangwon-do, ph (0361) 55-4409.

*Hanal*, 730-1 Onch'on-ri, Sangmo-myon, Chungwon-gun, Ch'ung ch'ongbuk-do, ph (0441) 846-3151/9.

*Sokrisan*, 3-8 Sangp'an-ri, Naesongni-myon, Poun-gun, Ch'ungch' ongbuk-do, ph (0433) 42-5211/5.

*Namju*, 52 Onch'on-ri, Sangmo-myon, Chungwon-gun, Ch'ungch' ongbuk-do, ph (0441) 846-0397/8.

# Spas

Hot springs, or spas, have long been popular with people suffering from a variety of illnesses. Korea has a number of hot springs that are well patronised. Following is a selection.

| Name | Location | Temperature°C |
|---|---|---|
| Ch'oksan | Nohak-dong, Sokch'o, Kangwon-do | 40-53 |
| Haeundae | Chung-dong, Haeundae-gu, Pusan | 42-60 |
| Ich'on | Anhung-ri, Ich'on-up, | |
| | Ichoon'gun, Kyongi-do | 30-35 |
| Kyongsan | Namsan-myon, Kyongsan-gun, | |
| | Kyongsangbuk-do | 26-29 |
| Magumsan | Puk-myon, Uich'ang-gun, | |
| | Kyongsangnam-do | 24-55 |
| Onyang | Onch'on-dong, Onyang, | |
| | Ch'ungch'ongnam-do | 30-57 |
| Osaek | Oga-ri, So-myon, Yangyang-gun, | |
| | Kangwon-do | 35-38 |

| Name | Location | Temperature°C |
|------|----------|---------------|
| Paegam | Onjong-myon, Ulchin-gun, Kyongsangnam-do | 30-53 |
| Pugok | Pugok-myon Ch'ungch'ongnam-do | 33-76 |
| Togo | Togo-myon, Asan-gun, Ch'ungch'ongnam-do | 25-27 |
| Tokku | Puk-myon, Ulchin-gun, Kyongsangbuk-do | 37-40 |
| Toksan | Toksan-myon, Yesan-gun, Chungch'ongnam-do | 31-45 |
| Tongnae | Onch'on-dong, Tongnae-gu, Pusan | 31-63 |
| Suanbo | Onch'on-dong, Sangmo-myon, Chungwon-gun, Ch'ungchongbuk-do | 50-52 |
| Yusong | Onch'on-dong, Chung-gu, Taejon, Ch'ungch'ongnam-do | 25-53. |

# Yogwans

Budget watchers may enjoy the hospitality of a Korean-style inn called a *yogwan*. They provide a mattress, called *yo*, a quilt (*ibul*), and a hard pillow stuffed with wheat husks (*pyogae*). In cold weather the room is heated by the unique *ondol* heated floor. For an additional charge, meals can be served in your room. Today some yogwans have beds, private bathrooms, hot water and colour TV. Room rates are from W15,000-30,000. Check that they are recommended by the Seoul Metropolitan City Government as are those listed below.

*Kwung Pyung*, near Ulchiro 1-ga Stn line 2, ph (02) 778-0104.

*Dae Won*, behind Sejong Cultural Centre, ph (02) 738-4308.

*Dae Woo*, behind Seoul Plaza Hotel, ph (02) 755-8067.

*Mun Hwa*, near Secret Garden, ph (02) 765-4659.

*Chong Gak Jang*, near Chonggak Stn line 1.

*Emerald*, near T'apkol Park, ph (02) 743-2001.

*O Bok*, It'aewon, ph (02) 795-4628.

*Seoul House*, It'aewon, ph (02) 795-2266.

*Rainbow*, near Namyong Stn line 1, ph (02) 792-9993.

*Hanam*, behind Toksugung Palace, ph (02) 777 7181.

*Acts Guest House*, near Ch'ungjongno Stn line 2.

*Sung Do*, near Seoul Police Bureau, ph (02) 737-1056.

# Mountain Huts

These are found along mountain tracks in National Parks. They are usually open for the same length of time as the park. They are very basic, usually made of stone with a wooden floor for sleeping. There are no bedclothes provided so you have to take a sleeping bag. As there is no heating, it would be too cold to stay in one during the winter months. Most have a very limited supply of tinned food, candles and matches. As well as a sleeping bag, you will need to take a primus and food.

# Yoinsuk

These are about the same as a yogwan, but cheaper. They are in traditional-style houses that are run down and could do with a good deal of maintenance work. They are not very clean but most have a homely atmosphere. Signs are only written in Korean. The price is about W4500-5000.

# Minbak

These are rented rooms in private homes. They are usually found in rural areas where there isn't a Yogwan. You will have to ask the locals where to find one as they do not display signs. They do not have set rates either, so you will have to bargain, but do this before you agree to stay. Most will supply a simple meal for an extra charge, but these must be ordered in advance. Prices vary, but are usually about the same as the cheaper yogwans.

# Bath Houses

If you stay in a hut or one of the cheap places mentioned above, you will have to look for a public bath house. These are called *mogyokt'ang*, but you can find them by looking for a red sign with a bowl of steam coming from it. There is an entrance fee of roughly W1045, then an extra W2000 for one of the attendants to scrub you down. For another minimal charge you can have a small towel, a hair cut and dry, shoes cleaned and soft drinks.

*The procedure is:* first take off your shoes before you enter the changing room where you will be given a locker. The key is on a rubber band which fits around your wrist. Undress, then go to the tub room. Using a rubber bowl provided, take the hot water out of the tub and pour it all over yourself. Sit on the tiny stool and soap yourself, wash your hair, then rinse off all the soap. Now you are ready to jump into the tub. You can stay as long as your like or as long as you can stand the hot water. Get out and repeat the performance. After the second soak, try the cold water tub. Make sure you wash yourself well before you enter any of the tubs. You can keep repeating this for as long as you like.

Some bath houses have mineral spring water and this increases in heat as you soak. Most have showers where you can wash yourself down, and the better class baths have saunas. You must allow at least an hour to get your money's worth. It is recommended that you spend some time relaxing before you leave.

Heart patients are not advised to have these baths, and people with contagious skin diseases are prohibited from having one.

Bath houses are open 6am-8pm, and are closed one day a week.

This is one way of experiencing the Korean way of life. Most people find it fun, but it is not really recommended for women.

# Food and Entertainment

Korean food is spicy with a tantalising aroma. It has a rich nutritious content and is low in calories. Seasonings used are garlic, chilli pepper, scallions, soy sauce, fermented bean paste, ginger and sesame oil. Visors cannot claim to have been to Korea unless they have tried *kimch'i*, the famous cabbage dish which Koreans eat with almost anything. There are many varieties of this dish and those who are not accustomed to hot food should be cautious.

Dishes more acceptable to the Western palace are *kalbi*, and *pulgogi*. These two meat dishes are made from beef or pork and are served at most Korean dinner parties. *Kalbi* is similar to Chinese spare ribs, and *Pulgogi* is made from strips of meat marinated in garlic and other spices. Neither is very hot, and as they are cooked at the table over a charcoal fire, they resemble a barbecue. *T'aenung* in northern Seoul is the best place to eat this fare.

**Other popular dishes are:**
*Pibimpap*, a mixture of rice, vegetables, egg and chilli sauce.
*Toenjang-tchige*, a thick broth made from fermented bean paste and vegetables eaten with rice.
*Naengmyon*, chewy noodles eaten in cold broth, is popular in summer.
*Samgyet'ang*, made of chicken and ginseng, is good for your health.

### Table Manners
Korean food is not served in courses, instead all dishes are placed on the table at the same time. This style is called *hanjongshik*, and there is no set order in which to eat the food. There are usually several communal dishes so the guest is not obliged to finish his serving. The main dish ordered is almost always accompanied by rice, soup and several side dishes all of which are included in the price. Koreans eat their rice and soup with a spoon and side dishes with chop sticks.

# Restaurants

## *Seoul*
### Korean

*Cheonha Jang Sa* 105-1′59 Kongdok-dong, Map′o-gu, ph (02)713-4131.

*Cheong Poong,* 99 Ikson-dong, Chongno-gu, ph (02) 765-0101/3.

*Chong Woon Gak,* 9 Muak-dong, Chongno-gu, ph (02) 735-2444.

*Dae Ha,* 50 Ikson-dong, Chongno-gu, ph (02) 765-1151.

*IDae Lim Jung,* 13-18 Pil-dong 2-ga, Chung-gu, ph (02) 266-1540.

*Daewon,* 89-10 Nonhyon-dong, Kangnam-gu, ph (02) 548-0323/7.

*Dae Won Gak,* 323 Songbuk-dong, Songbuk-gu, ph (02) 762-2818.

*Da Rae Won,* 258-59 It′aewon-dong, Yongsan-gu, ph (02) 793-3615.

*Da Sung,* 85-18 Kyonji-dong, Chongno-gu, ph (02) 733-7900.

*Geo Goo Jang,* 63-14 Sinsu-dong, Map′o-gu, ph (02) 715-3600.

*Gohyang Sanchon,* 260-6 Wu-dong, Tobong-gu, ph (02) 906-0101/5.

*Hangarham* (DLI 63) 60 Youido-dong, Yongdungp′o-gu, ph (02) 789-5955.

*Han Il Hoe Kwan,* 1-4 Uijuro 1-ga, Chung-gu, ph (02) 730-3700.

*Heewon,* 120-13 Sosomun-dong, Chung-gu, ph (02) 753-0537.

*Hongneung Galbi Tamra,* 74-7 Nonhyon-dong, Kangnam-gu, ph (02) 515-7900.

*Ino Garden,* 5-5 Shinyong-dong, Chongno-gu, ph (02) 359-2333.

*Kayarang,* 239-4 It′aewon-dong, Yongsan-gu, ph (02) 797-4000.

*K.C.C.T Club,* 45 Namdaemunno 4-ga, Chung-gu, ph (02) 757-0757.

*Koindol,* 726-162 Hannam-dong, Yongsan-gu, ph (02) 797-9433/4.

*Korean House,* 80-2 Pil-dong, Chung-gu, ph (02) 266-9101.

*Koryo Samkyetang,* 55-3 Sosomun-dong, Chung-gu, ph (02) 752-2734.

*Ko Ryo Won,* 32-43 Songwol-dong, Chongno-gu, ph (02) 732-2444.

*Mirak Garden,* 686-25 Hannam-dong, Yongsan-gu, ph (02) 790-3637.

*Monnijo,* 60-1 Soch′o-dong, Soch′o-gu, ph (02) 562-5486.

*Myong-Moon House,* 121 Yongdap-dong, Songdong-gu, ph (02) 245-0335.

*Myong Woul,* 34 Ikson-dong, Chongno-gu, ph (02) 762-4071.

*Nak San Garden,* 1-36 Tongsung-dong, Chongno-gu, ph (02) 644-3401/2.

*Neul Born Gong Won,* 92-12 Nonhyon-dong, Kangnam-gu, ph (02) 543-8804/6.

*Oh Jin Am,* 34-6 Ikson-dong, Chongno-gu, ph (02) 765-4306.

*Pung Lim Gak,* 11-2 Kyobuk-dong, Chongno-gu, ph (02) 738-6601.

*Rai Pang Garden,* 66-24 Nonhyon-dong, Kangnam-gu, ph (02) 544-4844.
*River Garden,* 261-4 Yomch'ang-dong, Kangso-gu, ph (02) 696-4180.
*Roof Garden,* (DLI63) 60 Youido-dong, Yongdungp'o-gu, ph (02) 789-5967.
*Sambo Garden,* 867 Shingil-dong, Yongdungp'o-gu, ph (02) 844-3500.
*Sam Chong Gak,* 330-115 Songbuk-dong, Songbuk-gu, ph (02) 762-0151.
*Sam Won Garden,* 623-5 Shinsa-dong, Kangnam-gu, ph (02) 544-5351.
*San Jung,* 232-13 Nonhyon-dong, Kangnam-gu, ph (02) 517-0044.
*Sejeong,* 182-1 Puam-dong, Chongno-gu, ph (02) 730-1717.
*Sung San,* 421-1 Yonhui-dong, Sodaemun-gu, ph (02) 324-0909.
*Woo Jung,* 86-8 Nonhyon-dong, Kangnam-gu, ph (02) 542-1741.
*Woorijib,* 31-3 Songp'a-dong, Songp'a-gu, ph (02) 416-55517.

**Western**
*Adoro,* 45-12 Samsong-dong, Kangnam-gu, ph (02) 511-1532.
*Chateau,* 76 Ch'ongdam-dong Kangnam-gu, ph (02) 540-3340.
*Governors Chamber,* (DLI63)60 Youido-dong, Yongdungp'o-gu, ph (02) 789-5761
*Hanil Kimpo Restaurant,* 712-1 Panghwa-dong, Kangso-gu, ph (02) 662-0283.
*International Grill,* 150 Konghang-dong, Kangso-gu, ph (02) 662-1438.
*London Pub,* 37 Youido-dong, Yongdungp'o-gu, ph (02) 783-3877.
*Plaza Restaurant,* 28-1 Youido-dong, Yongdungp'o-gu, ph (02) 782-5376, 4171.
*Panda,* 368 Ch'ungjongno 3-ga, Sodaemun-gu, ph (02) 362-8495/6.
*Press Center Restaurant,* 31 T'aep'yongno 1-ga, Chung-gu,
ph (02) 731-7532.
*Rose Garden,* 755-13 Pangbae-dong, Soch'o-gu, ph (02) 537-1104.
*Seagrams,* 83-17 Nonhyon-dong, Kangnam-gu, ph (02) 548-6764.
*Seoul Plaza Hotel,* Railroad 112 Pongnae-dong 2-ga, Chung-gu, ph (O2) 771-22.
*63 Sky Lounge,* (DLI63) 60 Youido-dong, Yongdungp'o-gu, ph (02) 789-5904.
*The Tower Gourmet,* 20 Youido-dong, Yongdungp'o-gu, ph (02) 787-1210.
*Twin Palace,* 20 Youido-dong, Yongdungp'o-gu, ph (02) 787-1212.

*WTC Club Restaurant*, 159-1 Samsong-dong, Kangnam-gu, ph (02) 551-5440.

*Ashoka* (Indian), Hamilton Hotel, 119-25 It'aewon-dong, Yongsan-gu, ph (02) 794-1171.

*Athene* (French), 1362-26 Soch'o-dong, Soch'o-gu, ph (02) 411-2000.

*Babarinos* (Italian), 1451-34 Soch'o-dong, Soch'o-gu, ph (02) 521-8871.

*Casa Blanca* (American), 40-1 Chamshil-dong, Songp'a-gu, ph (02) 411-2000.

*Chalet* (Swiss), 104-4, It'aewon-dong, Yongsan-gu, ph (02) 795-1723.

*Crystal Palace* (English), 40-1 Chamshil-dong, Songp'a-gu, ph (02) 411-2000.

*Dong Shin Food* (Italian), 115-8 Nonhyon-dong, Kangnam-gu, ph (02)511-0900.

*Eltoro* (American), 599-19 Sinsa-dong, Kangnam-gu, ph (02) 545-9773.

*Grandma's Plaza* (Italian), 40-1 Chamshil-dong, Songp'a-gu, ph (02) 411-2000.

*L'Abri* (French), 1 Congno 1-ga, Chongno-gu, ph (02) 739-8830/1.

*La Cantina* (Italian), 50 Ulchiro 1-ga, Chung-gu, ph (02) 777-2579/81.

*La Cucina* (Italian), 258-7 It'aewon-dong, Yongsan-gu, ph (02) 798-1631.

*McDonalds* (American), 120 Namdaemunno 5-ga, Chung-gu, ph (02) 757-0131.

*Muse* (French), 630-19 Sinsa-dong, Kangnam-gu, ph (02) 549-8111/2.

*TGI Friday* (American), 949-1 Togok-dong, Kangnam-gu, ph (02) 565-2961.

## Japanese
*Dado*, 106 Nonhyon-dong, Kangnam-gu, ph (02) 643-8943.
*Dongho* 2-14 Ch'ongdam-dong, Kangnam-gu, ph (02) 543-9624.
*Semi*, 640-6 Shinsa-dong, Kangnam-gu, ph (02) 547-9111.
*Wako*, (DLI 63) 60 Youido-dong, Yongdungp'o-gu, ph (02) 789-5751.

## Chinese
*China City*, 563-33 Shinsa-dong, Kangnam-gu, ph (02) 548-2222.
*Daekwanwon*, 1-1 Hangangno 3-ga, Yongsan-gu, ph (02) 719-7000.
*Doriwon*, 20 Youido-dong, Yongdungp'o-gu, ph (02) 787-1220.
*Harimgak*, 188 Puam-dong, Chongno-gu, ph (02) 738-7410.

*Manrisung,* 355 Chungnim-dong, Chung-gu, ph (02) 312-3388.
*Paengni-Hyang,* (DLI63) 60 Youido-dong, Yongdungp'o-gu, ph (02) 789-5742.
*Shin Dong Yang,* 35-5 Youido-dong, Yongdungp'o-gu, ph (02) 782-1754.

### General
*Dongbang Restaurant,* 150 T'aep'yongno 2-ga, Chung-gu, ph (02) 233-3131.
*Kimpo Int'l Air Ent,* 150 Konghang-dong, Kangso-gu, ph (02) 664-9503.
*Samhwa Restaurant,* 20-7 Sogong-dong, Chung-gu, ph (02) 755-2801.
*63 Fountain Plaza,* (DLI63) 60 Youido-dong, Yongdungp'o-gu, ph (02) 789-5732.

## Pusan
### Korean
*Bu Kwang Garden* 1489-10 Chung 2-dong, Haeundae-gu, ph (051) 743-0041/3.
*Byul Chun Ji,* 199-8 Kwangan-dong, Nam-gu, ph (051) 753-0660.
*Chong Ran Gak,* 1010 Sujong-dong, Tong-gu, ph (051) 461-0666.
*Chun Hyang Won* 24 Ch'ochang-dong 4-ga, Chung-gu, ph (051) 257-0221.
*Gaya Restaurant,* 15-4 Chungang-dong 4-ga, Chung-gu, ph (051) 463-3277.
*Kaya Jung,* 106-8 Posu-dong 2-ga, Chung-gu, ph (051) 253-1168.
*Kyo Mok Jang,* 16 Pumin-dong 1-ga, So-gu, ph (051) 244-1297.
*Moon Viewing House,* 1489-1 Chung 2-dong, Haeundae-gu, ph (051) 742-3386/8.
*Mok Jang Won,* 682-2 Tongsam-dong, Yongdo-gu, ph (051) 415-5500.
*Ulsukdo Gal Bi,* 1149 Hadan-dong, Saha-gu, ph (051) 206-4324.
*Wol Goong* 80-6 Posu-dong 2-ga, Chung-gu, ph (051) 246-9374.
*Yong Kung* 17-2 Pumin-dong 2-ga, So-gu, ph (051) 246-9371.

### Western
*Airport Restaurant,* 527-19 Taejo 2-dong, Kangso-gu, ph (051) 98-0088.
*Azellia,* 1533-4 Chung-dong, Haeundae-gu, ph (051) 743-6644.
*Chung Tap Grill* 36 Namp'o-dong 2-ga, Chung-gu, ph (051) 246-0071/5.

## Japanese
*Chungho Hoechip* 957-1-dong, Haeundae-gu, ph (051) 742-2946.
*Garden Eversea*, 13-1 Namp'o-dong, Chung-gu, ph (051) 247-2411/2.
*Goindol*, 596-1 Amnam-dong, So-gu, ph (051) 257-0262.
*Gyong Dong Jang*, 586-2 Amnam-dong, So-gu, ph (051) 244-7733.
*Hae Mi Rak*, 830-71 Pomil 2-dong, Tong-gu, ph (051) 644-23334/5.
*San Ho Ok*, 126-2 Amnam-dong, So-gu, ph (051) 256-3389.

## General
*Gon Po Garden*, San 19-3 Tongsam 1-dong, Yongdo-gu, ph (051) 414-0641/8.

## *Taegu*
### Korean
*Family Buffet*, 1623-12 Taemyong-dong, Nam-gu, ph (053) 654-9000.
*Hoe Jun Restaurant* San 302-11 Turyu-dong, Talso-gu, ph (053) 620-0300.

### Western
*Encore American*,195 Tongsongno 3-ga, Chung-gu,ph (053) 422-9600.

## *Kwangju*
### Korean
*Sukung Kalbi* 9 Ku-dong, So-gu, ph (062) 672-3511.

### Western
*J.J Machoneey* (American), 57 Hwangkum-dong, Tong-gu, ph (062) 225-7198.
*La Rosa* (French), 20-2 Kumnamno 2-ga, Tong-gu, ph (062) 228-2005.
*Venecia* (Italian), 750-72 Hak-dong, Tong-gu, ph (062) 228-1333.

## *Taejon*
### Korean
*Do Sung*, 117-5 Pirae-dong, Daedok-gu, ph (042) 625-1400.
*Phungmyon Pulkalbi*, 458-4 Taehung-dong, Chung-gu, ph (042) 252-9280/1.
*Song Won Garden*, 162-6 Okgye-dong, Chung-gu, ph (042) 283-7273.

### Western
*Hill Top*, 65-1 Unhaeng-dong, Chung-gu, ph (042) 255-3865/6.
*Tong Hae Garden*, 548-11 Pongmyong-dong, Yusong-gu, ph (042) 825-1460.

### Kyonggi-do
**Korean**
*Gohyangchon* 28-4 Shingal-ri, Kihung-up, Yongin, ph (0331) 8-2035.

**Western**
*Athene* (French), 1117 Ingye-dong, Kwonson-gu, Suwon, ph (0331) 36-0123.

### Chollabuk-do
**Western**
*London Pub* 43-5 Taga-dong, 3-ga, Wansan-gu, Chongju, ph (0652) 85-8802.

### Kyongsangbuk-do
**Korean**
*Bu Sung Park* 350 Ha-dong, Kyongju, ph (0561) 746-1616.
*Cheon Ma Park*, 99 Hwangnam-dong, Kyongju, ph (0561) 43-0311.
*Ko Gu Jang*, 220 Shinp'yong-dong, Konggju, ph (0561) 745-7551.
*Kumho San Meek*, 455 Songchong-dong, Kumi, ph (0561) 52-1818.
*Samwon Garden*, 167-2 Hwangnam-dong, Kyongju, ph (0561) 2-9440.
*Silla*, 142-3 Hwangnam-dong, Kyongju, ph (0561) 749-7717.
*Tong Hae*, 207 Noso-dong, Kyongju, ph (0561) 3-1116.
*Tong Hwa House*, 436 Shinp'yong-dong, Kyongju, ph (0561) 745-8021.

### Kyongsangnam-do
**Korean**
*Kumho Garden*, 745-4 Ch'ongch'on-ri, Chillye-myon, Kimhae, ph (0525) 42-3008/10.
*Daepan*, 98-2 Chungang-dong, Ch'angwon, ph (0525) 45-6661.

### Cheju-do
**Korean**
*Sammi Restaurant*, 273-22 Yon-dong, Cheju, ph (064) 46-6241.
*Soojeon*, 282-55 Yo-dong, Cheju, ph (064) 42-0555.

**Japanese**
*Hea Jo Whoi Kwan*, 515-2 Yongdam, 3-dong, Cheju, ph (064) 42-8820.
*Chungmun Orange Park*, 550 Hoesu-dong, Sogwip'o, ph (064) 33-8693.

# Entertainment

There is much traditional culture, and Korean dancing and music can be seen at several tourist destinations. Lately there has been increasing influence from foreign countries, and there are now many venues offering everything from discotheques to classical concerts.

The popular places for an evening out are the Myong-dong, It'aewon and Yongdong districts of Seoul.

For current information a visitor should read one of the English language papers or consult the notice board in the Korean Tourist Information Centre.

### Theatres

Korea's music, dance and drama can be enjoyed at many theatres. One of the largest and most centrally located is the all-purpose Sejong Cultural centre. It has a large and small theatre and an exhibition hall where art displays are exhibited. International touring companies often perform here.

Other all-purpose theatres in Seoul include Hoam Art Hall, downtown, the National Theatre on the slopes of Mt Namsan, downtown, and the Seoul Arts centre in southern Seoul. All present various performing arts. The Hoam Art Hall also shows movies and art exhibitions. The National Theatre has a large, small and experimental theatre as well as an open-air stage. It also has a restaurant called Chihwaja, serving traditional royal cuisine. It is run by Prof Hwang Hye-song, designated a 'human cultural treasure', ph (02) 269 5834, fax (02) 268 3026. The Seoul Arts Centre comprises indoor and outdoor theatres, concert and art halls, an arts library and opera house, and the acoustics are highly praised. The centre is home to the National Classical Music Institute. The institute is dedicated to preserving traditional music, dance and drama. Regular performances are held every Saturday at 5pm from February to December.

Authentic Korean performances, especially folk music and dance, are best seen outdoors at a *madang*, an open-air stage. One is located at the National Theatre the other Seoul Nori Madang. It is located behind Lotte World in Chamshil, south-east Seoul, on the shores of Lake Sokch'onhosu. Lake performances at Seoul Noru-Madang are free. They are held every weekend afternoon and on public holidays from April to October.

The theatre restaurants at the Sheraton Walker Hill Hotel, Korea House and the smaller Sanch'on restaurant in Seoul, put on shows that give a good introduction to Korea's traditional music and dance. The other major theatre restaurants are Pan Korea and Kuk Il Kwan.

Along with the larger theatres, small theatres have flourished in response to the growing popularity of plays. These often experimental theatres are concentrated in two districts, Taehangno Street and Shinch'on. Taehangno Street, a fashionable district with the more 'arty' crowd is located near Hyehwa Underground station in downtown Seoul. It was once the site of Seoul National University. Now the street is lined with theatres, galleries and chic cafes. Shinch'on, a 10 minute train ride from city hall, is a student district with four universities. There are small theatres each seating about 150, which offer experimental dramas by new authors.

*Hoam Art Hall*, 7 Sunhwa-dong, Chung-gu, ph (02) 751 5132 (seats 950).

*Kayagum*, San-1 Kwangjang-dong, Songdong-gu, ph (02) 453 0121 (seats 780).

*Korea House*, 80-2 P'il-dong, Chung-gu, ph (02) 266 9101 (seats 195).

*Little Angeles Performing Arts Centre*, 25 Nung-dong, Songdong-gu, ph (02) 444 8221 (seats 1500).

*Mun-ye Theatre*, 1-130 Tongsung-dong, S0ch'o-gu, ph (02) 762 5231 (seats 709).

*Nampa Music Hall*, 8 Hannam-dong, Yongsan-gu, ph (02) 709 2669 (seats 786).

*National Classical Music Institute*, Soch'o-dong, Soch'o-gu, ph (02) 585 3151 (seats 520).

*National Theatre*, San 14-67, Changch'ung-dong 2 ga, Chung-gu, ph (02) 274 1151 (seats 1518).

*Ryu Kwan-soon Theatre*, 32 Chong-dong, Chung-gu, ph (02) 752 0543 (seats 2023).

*Sanchon*, 2-2 Kwanhun-dong, Chong-gu, ph (02) 735 0312 (seats 100).

Sejong Cultural Centre, 81-3 Sejongno, Chongno-gu, ph (02) 736 2720 (seats 4000).

*Seoul Arts Centre*, 700, Soch'0-dong, Songp'a-gu, ph (02) 580 1414.

*Seoul Nori Madang*, 47 Chamshil-dong, Songp'a-gu, ph (02) 414 1985 (seats 3000).

*Soong Eui Concert Hall*, 8-3 Yejang-dong, Chung-gu 7, ph (02) 752 8924 (seats 1990).

## Movies

Korea's movie theatres are concentrated around Myong-dong and near T'apkol Park, commonly known as Pagoda Park downtown. Advance ticket sales begin three days before the showing. Details of what's on can be found in the English language newspapers.

*Daehan*, 125 Ch'ungmuro 4-ga, Chung-gu, ph (02) 278 8171.
*Dansungsa*, 56 Myo-dong, Chongno-gu, ph (02) 764 3745.
*Kukdo*, 310 Ulchiro 4-ga, Chung-gu, ph (02) 266 1444.
*Hoam*, 7, Sunhwa-dong, Chung-gu, ph (02) 754 4231.
*Hollywood*, 284-6, Nagwon-dong, Chogno-gu, ph (02) 745 4231.
*Korea*, 50-14 Myong-dong 2-ga. Chung-gu, ph (02) 776 4273.
*Myeongho*, 18-5 Ch'o-dong, Chung-gu, ph (02) 274 2121.
*Myeonghwa*, 94-139, Yongdungp'0 2-ga, Yongdungp'0-gu, ph 677 1108.
*Cine House*, 91-6, Nomhyon-dong, Kangnam-gu, ph (02) 544 7171.
*Lotte World Cinema*, 40-1, Chamshil-dong, Songp'a-gu, ph (02) 417 0211.

## Museums

Korea's historic treasures and cultural legacies are on display at national museums throughout the country. They are open 9am-5pm daily. (Close 4pm November-February.)

About 50 universities and colleges, also some overseas, have museum collections. Private museums also open their doors to the public. It is preferred, especially for tour groups, to make appointments prior to a visit to university and private museums. The universities have restricted opening hours during vacations.

## Cultural Organisations

### Korea Foundation

The Korea Foundation, formally the International Cultural Society of Korea, is dedicated to promoting international exchanges of cultural programs and services to foster mutual understanding and friendship between Korean people and the rest of the world. The Foundation's many activities include sponsorship and participating in international conferences, seminars and research activities in Korea and abroad, supporting Korean studies overseas and distributing Korean study material and enhancing cooperation with major cultural and academic organisations of other countries. The Foundation endeavours to strengthen and enrich world culture and the welfare of all humankind.

The address is 5th Floor, Daewoo Building, 526 Namdaemunno 5-ga, Chung-gu, Seoul, ph (02) 753 3463, fax (02) 757 2049.

### Yejiwon

The Yejiwon Cultural Institute offers programs featuring traditional Korean culture such as the wedding ceremony, tea ceremony, flower arranging, calligraphy and the preparation of *kimch'i*. Special programs can be arranged, on request, for group tours. The address is San 5-19, Changch'ung-dong, 2-ga, Chung-gu, Seoul, ph (02) 253 2211/2, fax (02) 253 2213.

### Korea House

See *Food* and *Sightseeing* sections.

### Royal Asiatic Society

The Korea Branch of the Royal Asiatic Society was founded in 1900 and is now one of the largest chapters operating under the auspices of its parent organisation the Royal Asiatic Society of London. RAS of Korea has consistently endeavoured to enhance understanding of the arts, customs, history and literature of Korea and other Asian countries by sponsoring lecture tours and publications.

Bi-monthly lectures in English provide interested visitors with the opportunity to learn from scholars and other experts on Korean and Asian affairs. These lectures are free and everyone is encouraged to attend.

Tours are conducted from March to July and from the end of August to November.

Unlike many tour organisations RAS attempts to supply a family type, non-commercial atmosphere. The tours are open to all and the cost is kept to a minimum although it is 20% less for RAS members, who also have priority on the tour list. The RAS has an extensive publishing program which over the years has created an invaluable source of information on Korean history, culture and language.

Monographs, handbooks, guidebooks and translations by distinguished Korean and Western scholars attest to the Society's commitment to providing accurate knowledge about Korea in English. All publications are considerably discounted to members.

Membership is US$20 for those not residing in Korea. For further information contact the Royal Asiatic Society Korea Branch, GPO Box 255, Seoul, ph (02) 763 9483, fax (02) 766 3796.

### Night Clubs
These are located in hotels and are rather expensive. They combine dancing with floor shows and cabaret acts. There are many discotheques that cater for foreign visitors.

### Beer Halls
These have sprung up at a rapid rate of late, and are often decorated in a European style. Customers are expected to buy a meal or snacks with their beer. Cocktail lounges and bars are found in hotels. There are also some bars, not in hotels, that cater only for men but they are noisy and not recommended for overseas visitors.

### Coffee Shops
Called *tabang* in Korean. The price of a cup of coffee is high but customers can sit and talk as long as they wish. Koreans tend to meet their friends here rather than in their homes.

### Snacks
If you feel like something light to eat in a park or similar venue, there are plenty of bakeries where you can select some interesting morsels at a very reasonable price.

All 'corner stores' have soft drink cabinets.

### Casinos
Korea has several licensed casinos equipped with facilities for roulette, blackjack, poker and other games, but they are exclusively for foreigners. Most tourist hotels have what they call a "games room" for visitors who wish to gamble.

# Shopping

Korea is known as a shopping paradise, however, you could easily encounter language problems in markets and small shops. There are many duty free and department stores in the city where English is spoken by some of the staff. Items are usually cheaper at venues outside the capital, Seoul.

The most popular buys are ready-made and made-to-measure clothes. It is advisable to try on any garment before making the final payment. Sporting goods, including ski equipment and many other items, are reasonably priced. Leather and eel skin goods are popular. Furs are far cheaper than you would find at home but you must check that you are able to import an item of fur into your country. Jewellery, especially amethyst and smoky topaz are reasonable as they are mined in Korea. Jade is also a popular buy. The local white jade is available in attractive necklaces.

Antiques of cultural value are not allowed to be taken out of the country. Check with the Antiques Assessment Office, ph (02) 662-0106. The most sort-after goods are wooden chests and furniture from the Chòsan dynasty, and it is easy to find copies of genuine antiques. Other popular buys are brass-ware, bamboo-ware, dolls, embroidery, ginseng, lacquer-ware, paper masks, fans, kites and silk.

The most popular shopping district for tourists is **It'aewon,** south of Mt Namsan. Here you will find anything you need at a very low price.

**Insa-dong,** just west of T'apkol Park, has always been an artists' quarter. There are many private art galleries and antique stores. Browse in the shops then have some traditional Korean tea in one of the intimate cafés.

## Department Stores

Department stores are located close to the major downtown hotels, in the Myong-dong area. They have a fine selection, but prices are fixed. There are a few in southern Seoul, in residential areas like Youido, Yong-dong and Chamshil.

All the major cities have department stores, usually strategically placed near the hotels.

Although each store has an information desk, the clerk may not be able to speak English. It is unlikely that the salesgirl will understand you either, but if the store has a duty free section, there is always one English-speaking person in that department.

Department stores have money changing facilities and accept major credit cards.

# Markets

The two largest are Tongdaemun, better known as East Gate, and Namdaemun, known as South Gate. **Tongdaemun** is on Chongno Street and is the largest market in Korea. It covers an area of ten blocks and you are sure to find anything you want in this colourful place. It is closed on the first and third Sunday of the month.

**Namdaemun** is a few minutes walk from the deluxe hotels in the downtown area. It is a little smaller but you can buy anything from sun glasses to cut flowers. It is especially famous for its quality clothing. Closed on Sundays.

**Kyong-dong market** is near Chegi station on line 1. It is Korea's most famous Oriental medicine market. An adjacent alley sells spices, such as chilli and garlic.

**Hwanghak-dong Flea Market,** east of Tongdaemun on Ch'onggyech'on street, is a collection of shops and stalls selling everyday items. There are many second-hand electrical shops.

**Yongsan Electronic Goods Market**, located near Yongsan railroad station, is a specialist market in every kind of electronic goods. In all, there are 2700 stores. Closed first and third Sundays.

**Myong-dong** is the major shopping district for high quality clothes and shoes. It is also crowded with cafés, restaurants and discotheques. It is within easy walking distance of most major downtown hotels and is the place to go when you want to be seen "about town".

As the markets are so big, ask your hotel information desk if they can supply a map.

### Markets Outside Seoul

*Ich'on Pottery Village*, Ich'on, Kyonggi-di - open daily.
*Moran Market*, Songnam, Kyonggi-do - an ordinary rural market

that is open on the 4th, 9th, 14th, 19th and 24th day of each month.
*Kanghwa Market*, Kanghwado Island, Kyonggi-do - specialises in large rush mats and ginsengs - open 2nd, 7th, 12th, 17th, 22nd and 29th day of each month.
*Sorae Seafood Market*, Sorae, Inch'on - open daily.

### Major City Markets

*Chagalch'i Fish Market*, Pusan - open daily.
*Kyongju Folkcraft Market*, Kyongju - open daily.
*Yusong Market*, Taejon - an ordinary rural market that is open on the 4th, 9th, 19th, 24th and 29th day of each month.
*Kumsan Market*, Kumsan, Ch'ungch'ongnam-do - open on the 2nd 7th, 12th, 17th, 22nd and 27th day of each month.
*Hansan Market*, Hansan, Kyongsangnam-do - good for Ramie cloth - open on the 1st, 6th, 11th, 16th 21st and 26th day of each month.
*Kurye Market*, Kurye, Chollanam-do - has mountain vegetables and herbal medicines - open on the 3rd, 8th, 13th, 23rd and 28th day of each month.
*Tamyang Bamboo Market*, Tamyang, Chollanam-do - open on the 2nd, 7th, 12th, 17th, 22nd and 27th day of each month.
*Namwon Market*, Namwon, Chollabuk-do - wooden ware, brassware, fans, hanji (traditional paper) - open on the 4th, 9th, 14th, 19th, 24th and 29th day of each month.
*Andong Market*, Andong, Kyongsangbuk-do - hemp cloth, hahoe masks - open on the 2nd, 7th, 12, 17th, 22nd and 27th day of each month.

# Duty Free Shops

### Seoul

*KNTC* Kimpo International Airport.
*Donghwa*, 211 Sejomgo, Chongno-gu.
*International*, 159-1 Samsong-dong, Kamgnam-gu.
*Jindo*, 128-5 It'aewon-dong, Yongsan-gu.
*KAL*, 381 Namdaemunno 5-ga, Chung-gu.
*Lotte*, 1 Songong-dong, Chung-gu.
*Lotte World*, 40-1 Chamshil-dong, Chung-gu.
*Pagoda*, 112-1 Chokson-dong, Chongno-gu.
*Shilla*, 202 Changch'ung 2-ga, Chung-gu.
*Walker Hill*, San 21 Kwangjang-dong, Songdong-gu.
*World Korea*, 77 Mugyo-dong, Chung-gu.

### Inch'on
*KNTC*, Inch'on International Seaport.

### Pusan
*KNTC*, Kimhae International Airport; Pukwan Ferry Terminal.
*Donghwa*, 69 Chungang-dong, Chung-gu.
*Paradise Nammun*, 1128-78 Chung-dong, Haeundae-gu.

### Cheju-do
*KNTC*, Cheju International Airport; Cheju International Seaport.
*Donghwa*, 263-15 Yon-dong, Cheju.
*KAL*, 292-53 Yon-dong, Cheju.
*Shilla*, 3039-3 Saektal-dong, Sogwip'o.

### Kyongju
*Donghwa*, 375 Shinp'yong-dong, Kyongju.
*Paradise Nammun*, 410 Shinp'yong-dong, Kyongju.

### Masan
*KNTC*, Masan International Ferry Terminal.

# Sport

## T'aekwondo

There are two traditional sports, T'aekwondo and Ssirum. **T'aekwondo**, a form of self defence, is an unarmed martial art that originated in Korea but is now practised all over the world. The World T'aekwondo Federation (WFT) has its headquarters in Seoul and hosts world championship competitions every two years. If you want more information, or to observe a competition, contact WFT at 635 Yoksam-dong, Kangnam-gu, Seoul, ph (02) 566-2525, or contact the Korea T'aekwondo Association on (02) 420-4271.

## Ssirum

The rules of **Ssirum**, Korean-style wrestling, state that if any part of the contestant's body, except the feet, touches the ground, then he is out. There are amateur and professional competitions throughout the year. Your hotel staff can assist you in attending a contest.

## Archery

Koreans have been noted for **archery** for centuries. A traditional Korean bow has a double curvature to maintain greater flexibility. Production of these bows is both complex and difficult. Western-style bows have been used more and more in recent years. The Korean Ssirum Association, The Korean Archery Association and the Korean T'aekwondo Association are under the control of the Korean Amateur Sport Association (KASA) which houses over 44 sport organisations. Its address is 88 Oryun-dong, Songp'a-gu, Seoul, ph (02) 420-3333, fax (02) 414-5583.

Modern sports include baseball, and it's easy to find a game in spring, summer and autumn. Soccer is also popular and there are many professional teams of high standard.

Other sports are tennis, table tennis, boxing, swimming, golfing, hunting, fishing, skiing, cycling and skating. Water sports such as yachting, wind-surfing, motor boating, water skiing and scuba diving can be enjoyed at the coastal resorts and on the Han-gang River in Seoul, although the south coast and Chejudo Island are the most suitable places for water sports. The water is at its warmest from June to September but comfortable for scuba diving until November.

Rental equipment is available, and most rental centres are found in coastal regions. Classes for beginners can also be arranged.

For more details contact the Korean Underwater Diving Association, 88-2 Dryun-dong, Songp'a-gu, Seoul, ph (02) 203-0488, fax (02) 413-0544; the Korean Water Ski Association 88-1 Dryun-dong, Songp'a-gu, Seoul, ph (02) 203-0488, fax (02) 413-0544; the Korean Yachting Association, Room 1807, Daewoo Building, 541 Namdaemunno 5-ga, Chung-gu, Seoul, ph (02) 773-8660, fax (02) 773-8660; and the Korean Wind-surfing Association, Room 402, Songhon Building, 55-3 Nonhyon-dong, Kangnam-gu, Seoul, ph (02) 511-7522, fax (02) 511-7523.

# Hunting

From November to February visitors are permitted to hunt on **Cheju-do** and **Koje-do Islands** and in one other mainland province. (The province changes from year to year). Game include wild boar, elk, rabbit, cock-pheasant, turtle-dove, duck and snipe.

The private *Daeyoo Hunting Club* runs a year-round hunting ground. It is located in the city of Sogwip'o, west of Chungman Resort on Cheju-do. It has more than 300,000 square metres (74 acres) of ground stocked with pheasant. Besides field hunting with a guide, it offers trap shooting and pistol practice. Other sports and conveniences are attached to the hunting ground - horse riding track, restaurant, shops, etc. Hunting equipment, dogs and rifles can be rented from the club and the hunting charge is W110,000 per person per day which includes guide, rifle and dog. For more information and reservations contact Cheju-do, 144 Sang-ye-dong, Sogwip'o, ph (064) 38-0500, fax (064) 38-5585.

The Korean Engineering Association of Explosives and Guns and Ammunition will help foreign hunters process clearance of guns and ammunition through customs. They also provide guns and hunting dogs. Interested parties are requested to contact the Association one month before arrival at 107-2 Shin-gil 2- dong,

Yongdungp'o-gu, Seoul, ph (02) 831-8152/8, fax (02) 831-8153.

# Fishing

Seashore or deep-sea fishing can be enjoyed at many locations along the coast and at Cheju-do Island and Hallyosudo Waterway. There are also fresh water lakes and reservoirs that offer good fishing spots. Various bus tour companies operate organised fishing trips. Contact your hotel information desk for reservations.

# Golf

A popular sport in Korea, there are over fifty excellent courses. Most tourist hotels in resort areas have their own or access to one. It is always advisable to book one week in advance through your hotel. One feature of golf courses in Korea is that they have facilities attached, such as lodging houses, youth hostels, tennis courts and outdoor swimming pools. There are major courses near Seoul, Kyongju and Cheju-do Island. Most are open from sunrise to sunset, although some courses have lights for night golf.   Each course charges slightly different **fees**, but average prices are:

Green Fees for non-members (including caddy fees) - weekdays W45,000, weekends W59,400. Caddie service (like a tip) - W20,000.

Rental of full set of clubs - W15,000. Golf shoes - W3,000. If you bring your own clubs, you must declare them at customson arrival.

## Golf Courses

**Seoul**
*Namsungdae* 419 Changi-dong, Songp'a-gu, ph (02) 403-0071/4 - 18 holes.
*Taenung (Yuksa)*, 230-30 Kongnung-dong, Nowon-gu, ph (02) 972-2111/4 - 18 holes.

**Pusan**
*Dongnae*, 128 Son-dong, Kumjong-gu, ph (051) 513-0101/4 - 18 holes.
*Pusan San*, 6 Nop'o-dong, Kumjong-gu, ph (051) 508-0707/10 - 18 holes.

**Taejon**
*Yusong*, 215-7 Tongmyong-dong, Yusong-gu, Taejon, ph (042)

822-7103/6 - 18 holes.

**Taegu**
*Palong*, San 1 Tohak-dong, Tong-gu, ph (053) 982-8080/5 - 18 holes.

**Inch'on**
*Inch'on Kukje*, 177-1 Kyongso-myon, So'gu, ph (032) 514-9991/4 - 18 holes.

**Kyonggi-do**
*Ansung*, 736-4 Changgye-ri, Ijuk-myon, Ansong-gun, ph (0334) 74-91211/7 - 18 holes.
*Anyang*, 1 Pugok-dong, Kump'o-shi, ph (0343) 62-0051 - 18 holes.
*Club 700*, San 11-1, Sanggu-ri, Taeshin-myon, Yoju-gun, ph (0337) 84-0701 - 18 holes.
*Dong Seoul*, 260-1 Kam 2-dong, Hanam-shi, ph (02) 470-2141/5 - 18 holes.
*Duckpyung*, 53-3 Maegok-ri, Hobop-myon, Ich'on-gun, ph (0336) 32-9623/7 - 18 holes.
*Gold*, San 18, Komak-ri, Khung-up, Yongin-gun, ph (0331) 283-8111/2 - 36 holes.
*Hanil*, San 69, Yanggwi-ri, Kihung-up, Yongin-gun, ph (0337) 84-7000 - 36 holes.
*Hansung*, 32-1 Pojong-ri, Kusong-myon, Yongin-gun, ph (0331) 284-3831 - 27 holes.
*Hawon*, 859-1 Puk-ri, Namsa-myon, Yongin-gun, ph (339) 73-7111/4 - 27 holes.
*Hanyang*, San 38-23 Wondang-dong, Koyang-shi, ph (02) 354-5000 - 36 holes.
*Ip'o*, San 1 Changhung-ri, Kumsa-myong, Yoju-gun, ph (0337) 84-3131/2 - 18 holes.
*Jaeil*, San 587 Pugok-dong, Ansan-shi, ph (0345) 82-8554/5 - 27 holes.
*Jungbu*, 28-1 Konijam-ri, Shilch'on-myon, Kwangju-gun, ph (0347) 62-6588/9 - 18 holes.
*Kihung*, 46 Shir-ri, Tongt'an-myon, Hwasong-gun, ph (0339) 72-4001/7 - 36 holes.
*Kumgang*, 1-2 Pondu-ri, Kanam-myon, Yoju-gun, ph (0337) 84-9951 - 18 holes.
*Kwanak*, San 22 Tongt'an-myon, Hwasong-gun, ph (0339) 72-6711/2 - 36 holes.

*Nambu,* 1-35 Pora-ri, Kihung-up, Yongin-gun, ph (0331) 281-8601/4 - 18 holes.
*Nam Seoul,* San 71-2 Paekhyon-dong, Songnam-shi, ph (02) 929-2611/3 - 18 holes.
Nam Suwon, 170 Songsan 1-ri, Taean-up, Hwasong-gun, ph (0331) 37-1201/2 - 18 holes.
*Nasan San,* 142-1 Kisan-ri, Ildong-myon, P'och'on-gun, ph (0357) 31-2003/6 - 18 holes.
*New Korea,* 227-12 Wondang-dong, Koyang-shi, ph (02) 352-0091 - 18 holes.
New Seoul, 1 Sam-ri, Kwangju-gun, ph (0347) 62-5672/5 - 36 holes.
*Palan,* 38-4 Haech'ang-ri, Palp'an-myon, Hwasong-gun, ph (0339) 52-5061/2 - 18 holes.
*Pal Pal (88),* San 80-2 Ch'ongdok-ri, Kusong-myon, Yongin-gun, ph (0331) 282-0881/3 - 36 holes.
*Plaza,* San 57 Pongmu-ri, Namsa-myon, Yongin-gun, ph (0335) 32-1122 - 36 holes.
*Royal,* 555 Mansong-ri, Chunae-myon, Yongin-gun, ph (0351) 40-1515/7 - 18 holes.
*Shinwon,* 49-1 Mong-ri, Idong-myon, Yongin-gun, ph (0335) 33-1800 - 18 holes.
*Suwon,* 313 Kugal-ri, Kihung-up, Yongin-gun, ph (0331) 281-6613/7 - 27 holes.
*Taegwang,* San 66 Shingal-ri, Kihung-up, Yongin-gun, ph (0331) 281-7111/5 - 27 holes.
*Yangji,* 34-1 Namgok-ri, Naesa-myon, Yongin-gun, ph (0335) 33-2001/3 - 27 holes.
*Yangju,* 300 Kumnam-ri, Hwado-myon, Namyangju-gun, ph (0346) 593-0561/2 - 18 holes.
*Yeojoo,* 35-10 Wolsong-ri, Yoju-up, Yoju-gun, ph (0337) 82-5881/2 - 27 holes.

**Kangwon-do**
Chuncheon, San 42-2 Chongjong-ri, Shindong-myon, Ch'unch'on-gun, ph (0361) 261-9417 - 27 holes.
*Sorak Plaza,* 24-8 Chagsa-dong, Sokch'o-shi, ph (0392) 635-7711/9 - 18 holes.
*Yongpyeong,* 130 Yongsan-ri, Toam-myon, P'yongch'ang-gun, ph (0374) 32-5757 - 18 holes.

## Ch'ungch'ongbuk-do
*Cheongju*, 40-1 Hwasan-ri, Och'ang-myon, Ch'ongwon-gun, ph (0431) 53-4818/9 - 18 holes.
*Chungang*, San 103-1 Songdae-ri, Paekkong-myon, Chinch'on-gun, ph (0434) 33-6667 - 18 holes.
*Chungju*, San 84-1 Wolsang-ri, Kumga-myon, Chungwon-gun, ph (0441) 848-0900/6 - 18 holes.

## Ch'ungch'ongnam-do
*Dogo*, 113-8 Shinsong-ri, Sonchang-myon, Asan-gun, ph (0418) 42-0271/3 - 18 holes.

## Chollabuk-do
*Iri*, San 226-1 Tokki-dong, Iri-shi, ph (0653) 856-2521/5 - 18 holes.

## Chollanam-do
*Kwangju*, San 166-1 Hapkang-ri, Okkwa-myon, Koksong-gun, ph (0688) 62-5533/5 - 18 holes.
*Nam Kwangju*, San 67 Yanggok-ri, Ch'unyang-myon, Hwasun-gun, ph (0612) 73-5511 - 18 holes.
*Sungju*, San 90-1 Tokchong-ri, Pyollang-myon, Sungju-gun, ph (0661) 741-4000 - 27 holes.

## Kyongsangbuk-do
*Kyongju Chosun*, San 13-1, Shinp'yong-dong, Kyongsan-gun, ph (0561) 745-7701 - 36 holes.
*Taegu*, 67-2 Sonhwa-ri, Chinyang-myon, Kyongsan-gun, ph (0541) 52-3011/4 - 27 holes.

## Kyongsangnam-do
*Bugok*, San 263 Komun-ri, Pugok-myon, Ch'angnyong-gun, ph (0559) 521-0707/10 - 18 holes.
*Changwon*, San 50 Pongnim-dong, Ch'angwon-shi, ph (0551) 521-0707/10 - 18 holes.
*Kaya*, San 1 Sambang-dong, Kimhae-shi, ph (0525) 33-009 1/4-36 holes.
*Tongdo*, 233 Tapkok-ri, Habuk-myong, Yangsan-gun, ph (051) 464-7751/5 - 36 holes.
*Ulsan*, San 105 Taedae-ri, Ungch'on-myon, Ulsan-gun, ph (0552) 68-0707/10 - 27 holes.

*Yongwon*, San 12 Yongwon-dong, Chinhae-shi, ph (0553) 41-0080 - 27 holes.

**Cheju-do**
*Cheju*, 2228-2 Yongp'yong dong, Cheju-shi, ph(064)56-0451/6 - 18 holes. *Chunggmun*, 2561 Saektal-dong, Sogwip'o, ph (064) 32-1202/4 - 18 holes. *Ora*, 289 Ora-dong, Cheju-si, ph (064) 47-5000 - 27 holes.

# Olympic Facilities

For the 1986 Asian Games and the 1988 Olympiad, Korea constructed sports facilities in Seoul, Pusan and Kwangju. The Seoul Olympic Organising Committee built 36 competition and 72 training venues to international standard. Eleven of the ultra modern facilities are located in the Seoul Sports Complex, 545,000 sq m, and Olympic Park.

The complex is only half an hour from downtown Seoul and 45 minutes from Kimpo International Airport by taxi. The Olympic stadium in the Seoul Olympic Complex covers 130,000 sq m and has a seating capacity of 100,000. Its shape was inspired by the graceful curves and lines of a porcelain vase of the Choson Dynasty. The stadium is open to the public every day 9am-6pm March-October, 9am-5pm November-February. Admission is W200. The visitors centre in the Olympic stadium presents slide shows describing the facilities in English. Foreign visitors are also treated to an escorted tour of the complex with an English speaking guide. The address is 10 Chamshil-dong, Songp'a-gu, Seoul, ph (02) 417-8807, fax (02) 418-8010.

The Olympic Park is 10 minutes by taxi from the sports complex. It accommodates an Olympic velodrome, weight lifting, gymnastics hall, fencing, tennis courts, gymnasium and the Olympic indoor swimming pool.

# Skiing

This is also a popular sport. There are eight resort areas within easy reach of Seoul. They have well groomed slopes, lifts, equipment for rent and ski schools for both group and private lessons. Accommodation is of high standard and there is plenty of night life. Reservations from overseas visitors will be accepted at the beginning of October. Domestic reservations from November. For more information contact each ski resort. Travel agents in Seoul arrange transport to and from resorts by tour bus.

### Ski Resorts

*Alps* - north of Mt Soraksan National Park, 3½ hours from Seoul by bus or car; 40 minutes by air from Seoul to Sokch'o, 40 minutes by shuttle bus to resort.

8 slopes (550-2200m), 5 chair lifts (W20,000), ski rental (W21,100).

1 hotel (48 rooms) - W45,000-60,000 (US$70-94); 1 family hotel (104 rooms) - W85,000 (US$133); 1 lodge (39 rooms) - W40,000-60,000 (US$62-94); 1 condominium (500 rooms) - W85,000-225,000 (US$133-353).

This field has the longest skiing season in Korea (early December - late March). Facilities include floodlit slopes for night skiing and a ski museum.

Resort address - San 1-2, Hul 1-ri, Kansong-up, Kosong-gun, Kangwon-do, ph (0392) 681 5030/9, fax (0392) 681 2788.

Seoul Office - Room 520, Sung Chang Building, 60-3 Ch'ungmuro 2-ga, Chung-gu, ph (02) 756 5481/2, fax (02) 754 3785.

*Bears Town* - north-east of Seoul, 50 minutes by bus or car to Naech'on, 5 minutes by taxi to resort.

7 slopes (500-2500m), 5 chair lifts, 2 T-bars (W20,000), ski rental (W22,600)

1 hostel (48 rooms) - W50,000-80,000 (US$78-125); 2 condominiums (337 rooms) - W76,000-114,000 (US$119-179).

The advantages of this field are its proximity to Seoul and its internationally recognised slopes of varying difficulty.

Resort address - 295 Sohak-ri, Naech'on-myon, P'och'on-gun, Kyonggi-do, ph (0357) 32 2534, fax (0357) 33-8427.

Seoul Office - Room 606, Dankook Building, 97 Nonhyon-dong, Kangnam-gu, ph (02) 546 7210, fax (02) 549 6719.

*Chonmasan* - north-east of Seoul, one hour by bus, car or train to Masok, then 7 minutes by taxi to resort.

5 slopes (700-1300m), 6 chair lifts, 2 T-bars (W20,000), ski rental (W20,000).

1 hotel (38 rooms) - W55,000-198,000 (US$86-310).

Also close to Seoul, this field has all-season artificial snow.

Resort address - 548 Muk'yon-ri, Hwado-myon, Namyangju, Kyonggi-do, ph (02) 233 5311/4, fax (02) 233 5311.

Seoul Office - 1-45 Tongsung-dong, Chongno-gu, ph (02) 744 6019, fax (02) 744 4788.

*Muju* - in Mt Togyusan National Park, 3½ hours from Seoul Office by shuttle bus to resort; 2½ hours by train to Yongdong, then ½ hour by shuttle bus; 3½ hours by bus from Nambu Terminal, Seoul, to Yongdong, then ½ by shuttle bus to resort.
17 slopes (90-3220m), 8 chair lifts, 1 J-bar (W23,600), ski rental (W22,300).
1 family hotel (742 rooms) - W145,200-326,700 (US$228-513).
This field has the longest ski slope in Korea, and a ski jump. Recreational facilities include paragliding, duck racing and physical endurance trials.
Resort address - San 43-15 Shimgok-ri, Soch'on-myon, Muju-gun, Chollabuk-do, ph (0657) 324 9000, fax (0657) 324 4993.
Seoul Office - 62-2 Nonhyon-dong, Kangnam-gu, ph (02) 515 5050, fax (02) 515 1127.

*Suanbo Aurora Valley* - near Suanbo Hot Springs, 2½ hours from Seoul by bus to Suanbo, then 5 minutes by taxi to resort.
7 slopes (250-1600m), 3 chair lifts, 1 T-bar (W15,700), ski rental (W16,000)
1 hotel (60 rooms) - W48,400 (US$76).
Resort address - San 54 Onch'on-ri, Sangmo-myon, Chungwon-gun, Ch'ungch'ongbuk-do, ph (0441) 846 0390, fax (0441) 846 0396.

*Yangji* - near Korean Folk Village, 40 minutes from Seoul by bus to Yangji, then 5 minutes by shuttle bus to resort (this bus is arranged by calling the resort from the Yangji interchange).
7 slopes (500-1500m), 4 chair lifts, 2 J-bars (W19,500), ski rental (W22,000).
1 hotel (60 rooms) - W60,000-100,000 (US$94-157).
The field is close to Seoul, and has Korea's first snow-making machine, and a 27-hole golf course.
Resort address - 34-1 Namgok-ri, Naesa-myon, Yongin-gun, Kyonggi-do, ph (0335) 33 2001/4, fax (0335) 327897.
Seoul Office - Room 204, Songpa Building, 505 Shinsa-dong, Kangnam-gu, ph (02) 515 1020/1, fax (02) 512 3675.

*Yongpyeong (Dragon Valley)* - near East Coast, 3½ hours from Seoul by bus.

19 slopes (630-2200m), 13 chair lifts, 2 T-bars (W20,900), ski rental (W21,100).

1 hotel (191 rooms) - W102,500-484,000 (US$160-760).

This is Korea's largest and most established ski resort, and is home to an annual snow festival.

Resort address - 130 Yongsan-ri, Toam-myon, P'yongch'ang-gun, Kangwon-do, ph (0374) 32 5757, fax (0374) 32 5769.

Seoul Office - 847-3 Taech'i-dong, Kangnam-gu, ph (02) 561 6255, fax (02) 561 6272.

*Seoul* - in Mt Paekpongsan, 40 minutes from Seoul (Ch'oongnyang -ri) by bus.

4 slopes (290-910m), 3 chair lifts (W20,500), ski rental (W23,100).

1 family hotel (66 rooms) - rates upon application.

Resort address - San 37-18, Hopyong-dong, Mikum-shi, Kyonggi-do, ph (0346) 591 1230.

Seoul Office - 995-14 Taech'i-dong, Kangnam-gu, ph (02) 561 1230.

The ski season lasts from December to March, but there are year-round activities such as golf, swimming and tennis. There is a 10%-50% discount on accommodation during the "off" season.

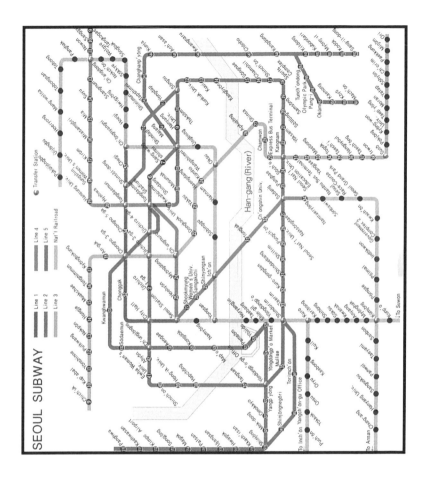

SEOUL SUBWAY

# Seoul

Some people prefer to make their own way to the sights, however, a guided tour is advantageous to give the visitor an idea of the layout of the area. They can then return later for a longer inspection if they wish.

It is advisable not to attempt more than one palace in a day. They are large, and there is a great deal to see and to absorb, so it can be tiring.

From the City Hall it is possible to walk to quite a few of the sites. Ask someone at your hotel to write down, in Korean, where you want to go. This is handy when asking for directions, using public transport, and hiring a taxi.

**Toksungung Palace** is just beside City Hall in the main downtown plaza. Five deluxe hotels, the Choson, Plaza, Lotte, President and Koreana are all within walking distance. The palace complex is dotted with commanding structures: *Taehanmun*, the main gate; *Chunghwajon*, the throne room; and *Sokchojon*, a Renaissance style building, the first of its kind in Korea. It now houses the Cultural Institute and offers monthly public audio-visual programs. The palace grounds are open all year round, 9am-6pm March-October, 9am-5pm November-February, closed Mondays. Admission is W550.

The **Anglican Cathedral**, built in 1926, is near Sejongno Street, north of Toksugung Palace and next to the British Embassy which was built in 1890. The Cathedral blends with the Victorian design of the embassy buildings. Services are held in both English and Korean.

**Kyongbokkung Palace**, at the northern end of Sejongno Street, was originally built in the late 14th century by the founder of the Choson Dynasty, but it has been rebuilt many times because of fire damage. *Kunjongjon*, the largest and most impressive building, was the throne chamber and audience hall. *Kyonghoeru*, a spacious two-storey pavilion, is situated over a pond near the throne hall. It was used to host feasts for royal ministers and diplomatic delegations. *Hyang-wonjong* is another secluded pavilion nestled in the middle of a lotus pond in the palace grounds. Royal families used the pavilion for small private parties.

Open 9am-5pm, closed Tuesdays. Admission is W550.

**The National Folklore Museum** is in the grounds of the Kyongbokkung Palace. It has many everyday items from the Choson Dynasty. Closed Tuesdays.

**The National Museum of Korea** stands just in front of the palace grounds. It has artefacts and relics that tell the story of 5000 years of culture on the Korean peninsular. Closed Mondays.

**Kwanghwamun Gate**, the former main entrance to the Kyongbokkung Palace, is now in front of the National Museum.

Turn east to **Ch'angdokkung Palace**, one of the favourite destinations for visitors. The main gate, *Tonhwamun*, is one of the oldest gates in the city. Near the entrance to the palace is the royal garage containing Korea's first motor vehicle. A must-see for antique car buffs.

**The Secret Garden**, *Piwon*, is a wooded garden tucked away in the corner of the Ch'angdokkung Palace. Its pavilions are interspersed with small streams and bridges. It is an oasis of exquisite beauty. In the past it was reserved for the royal family, but today, it is open to the public on a guided tour basis.

Daily tours in English at 11.30am, 1.30pm and 3.30pm.

Open 9am-5pm March-October, 9am-4pm November-February, closed Mondays. Admission is W1,800.

**Ch'anggyonggung Palace** is north-east of the Secret Garden. It has been restored, and the magnificent gates and elaborately arched bridges are well preserved.

Open 9am-6pm March-October, 9am-5pm November-February, closed Tuesdays. Entrance is W550.

**Chongmyo**, the Royal Shrine, is the resting place of the spirits of the Choson kings and queens. The grounds are open daily, but on the first Sunday in May, the courtyards and shrine buildings are open to the public for the annual Confucian ceremony *Chongmyo Taeje*. It is one of the most interesting and solemn ceremonies in Korea. (*see Festivals*)

Open 9am-6pm March-October, 9am-5pm November-February, closed Tuesdays. Admission is W550.

**Poshin-Gak,** a bell pavilion, is another landmark on Chongno Street. The original bell, cast in 1468, tolled the closing of the city gates at dusk and their opening at dawn, and is now in the National Museum. The replacement, dedicated in 1985, is tolled to ring in the New Year. The original bell is National Treasure no 2.

**T'apkol Park**, often called Pagoda Park, is on Chongno Street, and holds great significance in modern Korea. It was here on March 1 1919, that the Korean Declaration of Independence was read, followed by a series of peaceful demonstrations against Japanese colonial rule. The park was the site of the *Won-gaksa Temple* but all that remains of the temple is one pagoda, hence the name of the park.

**Children's Park**, in eastern Seoul, has thrilling rides, outdoor play areas, restaurants and a small zoo for the young.

**Tongdaemun**, the East Gate, is another main gate into Seoul, also from the Choson Dynasty. Its most distinctive feature is the defensive arrangement; a curving wall with an inner courtyard that has only one narrow entrance.

**Chogyesa Temple** is a large Buddhist temple near Insa-dong in downtown Seoul. It was selected as the headquarters of the Chogyejong Sect because of its central position. It is the focal point of the lantern parade on Buddha's Birthday.

**Myong-dong Cathedral** is located in the heart of Myong-dong. The interior of the cathedral is quaintly antique and has one of the few pipe organs in Seoul. It is famous for its Midnight Mass on Christmas Eve.

**Tongnimmun**, Independence Arch, was built in 1896 during Korea's opening up to the West. It is a symbol of the Korean people's determination to keep their country from foreign invasion and safeguard the national independence. It is located at a busy intersection north-west of downtown.

**Korea House**, near Ch'ungmro Subway station at the foot of Mt Namsan, is operated by the non-profit Foundation for Cultural Properties Preservation. It is an excellent example of traditional architecture. It has a restaurant serving authentic Korean food, a souvenir shop and a theatre that seats 195. It regularly stages a one-hour classical music and dance show, and is a favourite venue for Korean weddings.

Dance and music performances are staged at 7.20pm and 8.40pm, and cost W14,300.

Restaurant times are noon, 5.30pm, 7.30pm and 9.40pm.

Traditional set menus, *Hanjonghik*, cost W33,000, W44,000 and W55,000. The Korean buffet costs W19,800. The address is 80-2 Pil-dong, Chung-gu, Seoul, ph (02)266-9101, fax (02) 278-1776.

**Namsan** (South Mountain) was once south of the old capital but it has been engulfed by the city. It stands like a wooded island endeavouring to stem the urban encroachment, and its slopes are graced by deluxe hotels, such as the Sofitel Ambassador, Hilton, Hyatt, Shilla and Tower.

The mountain is a public park with a national theatre, and the **Botanical Gardens** are beautiful and well worth a visit. There are also statues of famous historical figures.

The interior of the mountain is criss-crossed by three tunnels that connect the city's northern and southern districts. Korea House stands on the northern side.

**Seoul Tower** with its TV transmission antenna, observation deck and revolving restaurant is on top of Mt Namsan. It is 480 metres high and offers a fantastic view of the whole of Seoul.

Open daily 10am-10.30pm, and admission is free. Entry to observation deck costs W1,300.

**Lotte World**, a mammoth leisure and shopping mall, is located in Chamshil. It comprises a deluxe hotel, folklore centre, indoor theme park, sports centre, a shopping mall and department stores.

The *Folk Village* is designed to give the visitor easy access to Korea's history and culture. The exhibition hall is in the form of a miniature village, performance hall and market place. The miniature village is remarkable in its reconstruction of the old way of life. In the market place, craftsmen demonstrate their delicate skills, and local products from all over the country are for sale.

*Lotte World Adventure* is a full-scale theme park with ultra-modern rides, puppet shows and parades. There are street scenes from all over the world. The indoor theme park is connected to the outdoor Magic Island, a theme park surrounded by Lake Sokch'onhosu behind Lotte World. Open all year Mon-Fri 9am-9pm, Sat-Sun and public holidays 9am-10pm. Admission is adult W5,000, child W3,000. A pass that includes all attractions is available for one day - adult W15,000, child W9,000.

Within the complex, there is also a sports centre with indoor swimming pool, bowling alley, ice rink and health club. For more information ph (02) 411-2000.

**Namdaemun**, Seoul's South Gate, stands amid heavy traffic near Seoul Railway Station, and is dwarfed by high-rise office buildings. It is just as imposing, however, as when it was first built in the late 14th century. It was then one of the main entrances to Seoul and was visible for miles around. It is National Treasure no 1.

**Seoul Nori Madang** is an outdoor theatre for traditional arts. It is located behind Lotte World on the shores of Lake Sokch'onhosu. Performances are usually free. Check the English daily newspapers for the program, or phone (02) 414-1985. Performances are held on Saturday and Sunday afternoons from April-October.

**The National Cemetery** lies in a valley that forms a natural amphitheatre. It stands on the southern side of the Han-gang River, west of the Seoul Express Bus Terminal. This is the final resting place of distinguished political and social leaders, military generals and war heroes. Special memorial services are held on June 6, Memorial Day.

**Seoul Grand Park** is an expansive parkland in the southern suburb of Kwach'on. It opened in 1984 with a zoo and dolphin show. Since then, it has added a Botanical Garden with 14,000 plants of 1,000 species, Seoul Land amusement park, and other facilities.

The **National Museum of Contemporary Art** is located beside the park. It is open 9am-7pm April—September, 9am-6pm October-March. Admission is W1150.

**Yejiwon Institute** was established in 1974 to revive the traditional female arts. Among the features are wedding ceremonies, tea ceremony, flower arranging, calligraphy and the preparation of *kimch'i*, the traditional dish. Special programs can be arranged for groups on request. Its aim is to share this unique culture with woman from all over the world and build up bonds of international understanding and friendship. Foreign visitors, both male and female, are welcome to visit the centre. For more information contact San 5-19 Changch'ung-dong, 2-ga, Chung-gu, Seoul, ph (02) 253-2211/2, fax (02) 253-2213.

**Youido Islet** is a reclaimed island in the Han-gang River that is now a government and financial centre. It is the home of the National Assembly, the Stock Exchange, many corporate bodies, Korea's three broadcasting stations, the DLI building, and the Full Gospel Church. Youido Plaza, in the centre of the island, is sometimes the site of outdoor gatherings but is mostly used by residents for cycling and roller skating.

Across the plaza from the Korean Broadcasting station is the Federation of Korean Industries Building which houses the Korean Industrial Exhibition Centre.

**DLI 63** (Daehan Life Insurance) building is one of the tallest in Asia. Visitors cannot help but notice the tall, golden structure as they travel from the airport to central Seoul. This sophisticated office building has many tourist attractions - the IMAX theatre, an aquarium, shopping mall and conference hall. For information ph (02) 789-5670.

# Outlying Attractions

### West

**Inch'on** is the major port near Seoul. It is situated in the low-lying area west of Seoul and is bordered by the West Sea and the Han-gang river.

It was through this port that Westerners first came to Korea in the late 19th century. It is also where General Douglas MacArthur led the UN troops in the famous Inch'on Landing in 1950 that turned the tide of the Korean War. It lead to the recapture of Seoul from the Communist forces. *Chayu (Freedom) Park*, on a small hillock overlooking the harbour, commemorates the success of this landing.

**Kanghwado** is Korea's fifth largest island. It is north of Inch'on where the Han-gang, Yesong-gang and Imjin-gang rivers meet. Today it is a serene island but in the past it played an historic part in resisting attempts by the west to open up the nation to foreign trade. During the Choson Dynasty the eastern side was heavily fortified, and was the most strategic point in the defence of Seoul. The ramparts have since been restored.

Local produce includes ginseng and rush mats, and ginseng farms can be found on the lower slopes of the island.

Inter-city buses connect Seoul with Kanghwado island, and they depart from Shinch'on in the western part of Seoul. The journey takes about 1 hour 10 minutes.

**Songdo Recreation Area** lies about 20 minutes south of Inch'on by taxi. It is ideal for picnics. There is boating on the lake and it is possible to observe wildlife.

**Yonan Breakwater**, on the southern outskirts of Inch'on, is a mecca for seafood lovers. There is a wide variety on offer including spicy clam soup and deep fried prawns. Most of the restaurants prepare and serve the food outdoors.

### South

**Ich'on** became a tourist spot when it was discovered that it was the place where the famous Choson white porcelain was made. The area is blessed with good clay and mineral-free water, vital elements for the production of quality pottery.

The highway from Ich'on to Kwangju is lined with kilns of well known Korean potters. They reproduce Choson porcelain and have rediscovered the art of making *Koryo* celadon.

Visitors have the opportunity to see the kilns and watch the production of the celadon and porcelain. You can save money by buying the pottery direct from the craftsmen.

The **Korean Folk Village** is just outside Suwon. Here in the farmhouses, homes of the nobility and other old-style buildings, you will find weavers, millers, potters, blacksmiths, pipe makers, and other craftsmen working in the way of their ancestors. You can buy traditional Korean handicrafts, and the restaurants serve regional food and drink.

Folk dances, musical performances and traditional ceremonies, such as weddings, take place in the village's small amphitheatre. Open daily 9am-5pm December-February, 9am-6pm March-November. Admission is W3,600.

**Yong-in Farmland** is Korea's answer to an African safari, although it also has a small carnival with roller coasters and a haunted house. The open zoo is an unforgettable experience. Visitors ride in a mini-bus through the zoo's natural animal environment.

The *Hoam Museum* displays a private art collection, and another attraction within the complex is *Global Village* which exhibits various cultural scenes from 21 different countries. Inside the building is a waterway lined with 1000 figures representing different parts of the world.

Open 9.30am - 6pm November - April, 9.30am - 9pm May - October. Admission is W3,200.

**Namhansansong Fortress** is the southern fortification for the defence of Seoul. It is located on the top of a hill near the southern satellite city of Songnam. It is a favourite picnic spot and gives a fine view from the summit.

**Suwon** is about a one hour drive south of Seoul, and the trip would not be complete without sampling *kalbi* (broiled beef ribs) at one of the restaurants. A special summer treat is to eat ice-cold watermelon or freshly picked strawberries and ice-cream. In autumn, sweet grapes are the specialty.

A narrow-gauge railway runs three times a day between Suwon and Inch'on (Songdo Station) taking farmers and their produce to the market. It is an ideal way to have a close-up view of the scenic, rural countryside. The railway dates from pre-industrial days when the government came to the aid of farmers by helping them to commute to and from the marketplace.

**Suwonsong Fortress**, with its artistically designed gates has been restored. It is now the main tourist attraction within Suwon. A limestone wall constructed in the 18th century runs between the gates, gun towers and command posts, and near the gates are modern pavilions where light beverages, snacks and souvenirs can be purchased.

**Shilluksa Temple** lies across the river from Yoju. It was built in 580AD, and is noted for its brick pagoda. A marble lantern and a tranquil gingko tree are especially enticing to picnickers.

**Yongnung,** located some distance from Yoju, is the burial ground of King Sejong. The tomb is in the typical style: a high mound with a granite altar guarded by carved stone statues of scholars and Chinese zodiac animals. There is a stone monument near the tomb that was carved in 1446 to announce the creation of the Korean writing system, largely due to King Sejong's efforts. His other inventions were numerous in the fields of science, music and literature, and his reign is considered to be the highlight of Korean culture. Each year, in mid-May, a Confucian ritual, King Sejong, *Sungmoje*, is held in his honour.

### North
**P'anmunjon** lies one hour north of Seoul in the Demilitarised Zone. (see *Tours*).

**Puk'ansansong Fortress** is the northern fortification for the city of Seoul. It encircles the peaks of Mt Samgaksan.

### East
The area east of Seoul lies in a series of hydro-electric dams on the Puk'an-gang River, which forms the Ch'ongp'yong, Uiam, Ch'un-ch'on and Hwach'on Reservoirs. There is also the beautiful Soyang-gang River Reservoir. These reservoirs have turned the area into a vast water vacation land. Pleasure boats cruise all the reservoirs and water-skiing, swimming, boating and fishing are all popular.

**Ch'unch'on** is the capital city of Kang-wondo Province and has some of Korea's most spectacular scenery. Called the "City of Lakes", it is almost completely surrounded by them.

**Namisom** is a small islet near Kap'yong on the Puk'an-gang River, half way between Seoul and Ch'unch'on, and it is another popular resort. Modern cabins, hotels, various recreational facilities and restaurants offer the perfect setting for a relaxing weekend.

**P'altang Reservoir** is a little closer to Seoul and lies where the north and south branches of the Han-gang river meet. People like to go sailing here in the summer.

**Yongmunsa Temple** stands near the P'altang Reservoir. It is the home of the world's largest gingko tree.

# East Coast Area

## Kangnung Area

*Kangnung City* lies at the end of the Yongdong Expressway. Before the expressway was built, the city was a small fishing village. Now it is an up-and-coming holiday resort. There is an historic building, *Ojuk'on*, where Yi Yul-gok, the great Confucian scholar of the Choson Dynasty lived with his mother, Shin Saimdang. She was the most famous woman of the Choson Dynasty, as she was a painter, calligrapher, poet, and an ideal wife, mother and daughter. Another interesting site is *Son-gyojang*, a nobleman's mansion built about 200 years ago. Continue south along the coastal highway.

## Samch'ok Area

Samch'ok has long been a major fishing village as well as the East Coast's chief shipping centre. There are many fine beaches in the area and several hot springs. Tokku and Paegam hot springs lie to the south of Samch'ok.

*Songnyugul Cave*, a 470m long limestone cavern, is full of stalactites and stalagmites.

*Mt Chuwangsan National Park* has an area of 103 sq km. It can be approached from either *P'ohang* at the southern end of the coastal highway, or by the steeper, more scenic route from *Andong*. *Yongdok*, a coastal town in the region, is famous for its delicious crabs. *Pogyongsa Temple* is worth a visit. It is the site of an historic stupa (a dome shaped Buddhist building for relics). There is an ancient mirror as well as several other treasures.

*P'ohang* is the home of Korea's largest steel mill, POSCO. Guided tours can be arranged for the visitor. P'ohang is a major shipping port and the terminal for the Ullungdo Island Ferry.

From P'ohang you must return to Kangnung, either by the coast road or the inland road.

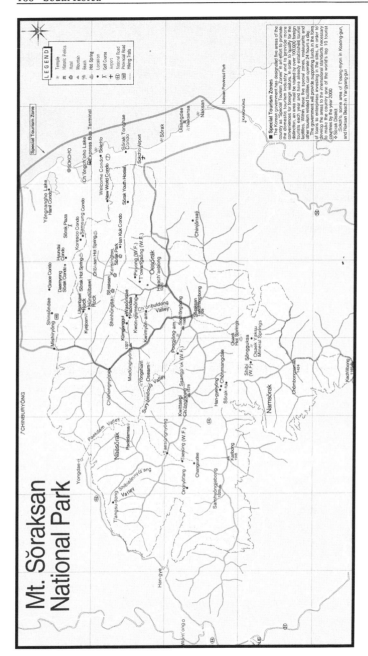

Do not think of driving too far northward from Kangnung or you will find yourself in North Korea.

*Kyongp'odae* is a well-known resort just north of Kangnung. The clean, white, sandy beaches with sparkling, blue water from the East Sea, have a border of silver spruce pine trees behind them. It is a delightful place all year round. In summer you can lie on the beach or swim in the clear water. You can also walk among the rocky crags of the East Coast, or visit nearby historic sites, or take a pleasant drive to Mt Soraksan, only an hour away.

In winter Kyongp'odae is a winter wonderland with snow drifts. The snow-covered pine trees magnify the brilliance of the sunrise.

*Kyongp'odea Pavilion*, on the hillside near the Kyongp'odae beach, is one of the most famous places on the East Coast. The wooden structure was originally built elsewhere in 1326, during the Koryo Dynasty, and moved to its present site during the Choson Dynasty, 1392-1910.

*Mt Odaesan National Park* is 300 sq km in area, and can be reached by turning off the Yongdong Expressway before Taegwallyong Pass and heading north.

The *Wolchongsa Temple* is one of the oldest temples from the Shilla Period, although it has been destroyed by fire and rebuilt many times. Within the temple compound is an eight-sided, nine storey stone pagoda. It was constructed by a monk, Chajang, during the Shilla Kingdom.

The *Yongpyeong Dragon Valley Ski Resort* is just outside the Mt Odaesan National Park near the Taegwallyong Pass. It is a fully equipped resort and has superb skiing.

*Mt Soraksan National Park* is 354 sq km of rugged beauty. There are fantastic rock formations, lakes and waterfalls. All these scenic landmarks are described in legend and myth. The park is divided into the inner area and the outer. The more rugged Inner Sorak (*Nae Sorak*) lies to the west of the highest Taech'ongbong Peak, the ridge of Han-gyeryong Pass. The Outer Sorak (*Woe Sorak*) stretches east of the village of Sorak-dong.

*Han-gyeryong Pass*, literally "Cold Valley Pass", forms the dividing line between Inner and Outer Sorak. Previously, it was called Osaengnyong Pass, "Five-colour Pass", because of its rich and colourful landscape.

*Changsudae Villa,* east of Ongnyot'ang in Inner Sorak, was constructed in 1958, by soldiers, to honour the victims of the Korean War. The villa also serves as a rest area for travellers.

*Paektamsa Temple* is at the western edge of Inner Sorak. It is one of the first sights visitors encounter on entering the park from Inje.

*Taesung Waterfall,* in Inner Sorak, is one of the three highest in Korea. *Ongnyo-t'ang,* in the same area, is known for a fascinating story. According to the legend, a heavenly spirit was attacked by a monster and sought refuge at the waterfall. A god hurled a lightning bolt at the monster to save the angel.

*Osaek Mineral Water,* a name derived from a word that means "five colours", is a famous product of Mt Soraksan. In Inner Sorak there is a spring which produces 1500 litres of mineral water a day. It was discovered by a monk from the Osaeksoksa Temple who described the place as "very beautiful where trees bloomed". Many people think the water relieves digestive ailments, skin diseases and nervous disorders.

*Ch'onbultong Valley,* in Outer Sorak, appears as if it is something straight out of a fantasy because of its unusual stone formations. These resemble a variety of human and animal shapes.

*Hundulbawi Rock,* the "Rocking Rock", is a huge boulder which can be rocked by a person of average strength, but it is impossible to shift it from its original position. The rock is situated to the north of Shinhungsa Temple in Outer Sorak.

*Kumganggul Cave,* 3.4 km from Sorak-dong in Outer Sorak, contains some Buddhist statues and the remains of earthenware utensils and tools. It was possibly inhabited by monks in the past.

*Kwon-gumsong Fortress* is perched on the top of a peak in Outer Sorak. It is surrounded by a 2 km long stone wall completed during the Shilla period. The fortress can be reached by the 1,100m cable car from Sorak-dong in the floor of the valley.

*Kyejoam Hermitage* is close to Hundulbawi Rock in Outer Sorak. It is the site of a seated Buddha.

*Piryong* and *T'owangsong Waterfalls* are in Outer Sorak and are famous for their beautiful rainbows.

*Pisondae Plateau* is an interesting tourist site in Outer Sorak. Legend has it that an angel ascended into Heaven from here.

*Shinhungsa Temple* is a 0.6 km walk from Sorak-dong village in Outer Sorak. It was first built in 653AD. Burnt down in 1645 it was rebuilt.

*Sorak-Dong* is the village located at the base of Mt Soraksan and is the entrance to Outer Sorak. It was developed as a resort village and is the starting point of the climbing trails. Inns, hotels, shops, car parks and camping sites are abundant.

# Sokch'o Area

The city of Sokch'o can be reached from Seoul via Highway 44 in about five hours. You can also fly to Sokch'o in under an hour. It acts as a gateway to Mt Soraksan National Park, and the entrance to the park lies ten minutes south along Highway 44. Sokch'o, like many of the towns and cities of the East Coast, is also a major fishing port where you will see racks of fish drying in the sun. The harbour is astir with the hustle and bustle of fishermen. This is a good place to stop, relax and dine after the long trip from Seoul. Abalone porridge, prepared from a recipe handed down for centuries, is served in the outdoor restaurants on the wharf.

*Naksansa Temple,* to the south of Sokch'o, was established by the renowned monk, Uisang, after he had obtained enlightenment. A 16m statue of the Buddhist Goddess of Mercy looks out over the sea. The local people pray to her for the safe return of the fishermen.

*Uisangdae Pavilion* lies near Naksansa Temple. Large numbers of visitors flock to the pavilion at dawn to see the sun rise. The pavilion is set amongst ancient pine trees, and is at its most beautiful when the sea mists are dispersed by the morning sun.

*Ch'oksan Hot Springs,* just outside Sokch'o, is a newly-opened resort with an hotel and excellent spa facilities.

The *Alps Ski Resort* is 45 minutes by bus to the north-west of Sokch'o, in Chinburyong Pass. This is Korea's northernmost ski resort and has snow for the longest duration. The season begins early December and lasts until late March. (see *Ski Resorts*)

The *Unification Observatory* is in the north of the Uisangdae Pavilion. On a clear day you can see Mt Kumgangsan in North Korea. The observatory is a symbol of the Korean people's long-cherished desire for the re-unification of the two Koreas.

*Hwajinp'o Beach,* the northernmost public beach on the East Coast, is one of Korea's most beautiful and unspoiled places.

# Ullungdo and Tokto Islands

Ullungdo Island lies 268 km north-east of P'ohang. It is an extinct volcano that rises steeply out of the East Sea. It is home to two hardy fishing villages. Though the terrain is steep and rocky, Ullungdo Island is a lush place in summer. Its clear waters are as beautiful as those around the Mediterranean islands.

The Tokto Islands, the most easterly point of Korea, lie 92 km to the south-east of Ullungdo. They are just two rocky outcrops.

# Central Area

Taejon, Ch'ungju, Kimch'on, Andong, Yongju and Ch'ongju are the principal cities. The central area has an extensive bus and railway network, making it easy for visitors to travel around. There are also four national parks: Mt Sobaeksan, Mt Woraksan, Mt Sobaeksan and Mt Kyeryongsan. They are noted for their natural beauty and historic temples.

# Andong Area

Andong can be reached by train from Ch'ongnyangni station in Seoul. The Ardong-Yongju region is a stronghold of Confucianism. The visitor can see old people dressed in the horsehair hats and traditional costumes of their ancestors.

*Andong Dam and Reservoir* are on the outskirts of the town and are being developed into a resort area.

*Hahoe Maul* (Andong Folk Village) has been protected by the government to preserve the architecture and Confucian heritage which dates back to the Choson period 1392-1910. The village is also famous for its unique mask dance which is performed at the well-known Pyolshin-kut Ritual.

*Tosan Sowon*, an hour's drive from Andong, is the Confucian institute founded by the great scholar Yi Toegye in 1560. In the seclusion of a densely wooded mountain, scholars devoted their energy to learning the wisdom of the classics.

*Chikchisa Temple* lies near the city of Kimch'on on the Seoul-Pusan expressway. The outstanding features of this temple are the blue-tiled roof of the main building and the thousand statuettes of Buddha as a baby. The support pillars of the main gate are made from a thousand-year-old tree. The temple is especially beautiful in autumn when the colours are at their best.

## Ch'ungju and Tanyang Area

*Ch'ungju Reservoir*, on the outskirts of the town, transformed 52 sq km (20 sq miles) of rocky farmland into a beautiful lake. Here you can enjoy a variety of water sports including water-skiing, boating and fishing. Luxurious air-conditioned boats cruise between Ch'ungju and Tanyang at the eastern end of the lake.

*T'an-Gumdae* is another beautiful place near Ch'ungjuho Lake. It is where the well known musician Uruk of the Shilla Kingdom trained his disciples in musical techniques. 'T'an' means to play a musical instrument and 'gum' is a type of zither developed during the Kaya Kingdom. The instrument is called kayagum.

*Tanyang*, at the eastern end of Lake Ch'ungjuho, is a limestone area. It has many natural sights including the 'Eight Scenic Wonders of the Tanyang Area', which are outstanding examples of the strange formations caused by limestone erosion. There are also a great many caves, the most famous being Kosudonggul, ('Underground Palace'), less than one mile from Tanyang city centre. It contains glittering stalactites in all shapes and sizes.

## Mt Songnisan National Park

*The Emileh Museum* is near the national park, and houses a fine collection of Korean folk paintings.

*Popchusa Temple*, inside the park, was first established in 553AD and has several works of art. The temple's most striking feature is the 33m high (108 feet) statue of the 'Buddha of the Future'. It was cast in one mould and is the largest standing bronze Buddhist figure in the Orient.

## Taejon Area

Taejon was the site of the Taejon Expo '93. It is about two hours south of Seoul and can be reached by bus or train. It is the main train junction for the Seoul-Pusan and Seoul-Kwangju-Mokp'o-Yosu lines.
*Yusong Hot Spring* is just west of the city and is considered one of the finest in Korea.

*Mt Kyeryongsan*, west of Taejon, has long been the home of a variety of religious sects that blend: Shamanism, Buddhism, the tenets of Confucianism and even Christianity.

Mt Kyeryongsan is also the site of Kapsa and Tonghaksa Temples. Tonghaksa is one of the few Korean temples that function as a convent for female monks. There are numerous hiking trails which are particularly beautiful in Autumn.

# Yongju Area

Yongju is one of the main railway junctions on the way to Kangnung. Like Andong it is still very Confucian in its traditions.

*Mt Sobaeksan* (1,439m) soars up at the beginning of the Sobaeksanmaek Mountain Range. Nearby is *Pusoksa Temple* which has some of the oldest wooden architecture in Korea, and is of special interest. It can be reached by bus from downtown Yongju and the trip takes about an hour.

The temple was founded by the great monk Uisang, who also established Naksansa Temple south of Sokch'o. He is credited with introducing the Hwaomjong Sect of Buddhism from China. The Muryang-sujon Pavilion within the temple, is believed to be the oldest existing wooden structure in Korea. The seated image of the Buddha enshrined in the hall, dates back to the Koryo Period. The murals in the main hall are the oldest of their kind in Korea.

# West Plain and Coastal Area

The area covers Korea's three south-western provinces, Chollanam-do, Chollabuk and Ch'ungch'ongnam-do. The region is rugged and mountainous with broad stretches of rice paddies.

*Honam Plain*, the rice producing area is often referred to as the 'rice bin of Korea'.

Paekche, one of the three ancient kingdoms of Korea, is known to have extended its influence from Seoul to the tip of the south-western peninsula. In its heyday, the Paekche Kingdom developed its own distinctive culture and artistic styles. They passed on this culture to Japan, influencing the Japanese in ceramic techniques and design, sculpture, handicrafts and tomb construction. The area is now being developed for tourism with emphasis on the historic remains of the Paekche Kingdom.

If driving south from Seoul, you will come to the Ch'onan area. If going by ferry, Mokp'o will be your port on the north-west coast.

*Mokp'o* lies just south-west of Kwangju and is the main ferry terminal for islands off the south-western coast, and Cheju-do and Hongdo Islands.

Travel east and you come to the Onyang area.

# T'aean Haean National Park

T'aean Peninsula, and the coastal area beyond, is located in the north-western part of Ch'ungch'ongnam-do Province. T'aean is the last major bus terminal for this coastal area and there are several worthwhile excursions from the town.

*Anmyondo Island* has distinctive flora and is famous for its camellias.

*Mallip'o Beach* is one of Korea's finest sandy beaches.

*Yonp'o Beach* is ideal for swimming and sailing.

# Onyang Area

Onyang is a hot spring resort just an hour's drive from Seoul. The spa's fame for medical properties dates back 600 years. Onyang's other claim to fame is as the home town of Korea's greatest military hero Admiral Yi Sun-shin.

*Hyonch'ungsa Shrine* was set up by the government in honour of Admiral Yi Sun-shin. The large shrine compound includes the hillside sanctum, a museum of the Admiral's relics, as well as modern paintings of his victories. The archery range was used by him as a young man. The compound also includes gardens with beautifully landscaped lawns and an artificial lake.

The *Onyang Folklore Museum* is another favourite with tourists. It has many folk items and crafts which illustrate many aspects of daily life.

# Ch'onan Area

The *Great Buddha of Mt T'aejosan* in Ch'onan is the largest gilt-bronze sitting Buddha of its kind in the Orient and is 14.2m high (46 ft) 10m (32 ft) in diameter. It was erected as a prayer for the unification of Korea in 1977.

*The Independence Hall of Korea* is to the east of Ch'onan on the other side of the Seoul-Pusan expressway. It honours all those who have struggled for freedom against foreign invading forces throughout Korea's long history. The memorial hall collects, studies and exhibits historic artefacts and materials related to the Korean national resistance, the fight for independence and the search for a national identity. It also keeps records of the nation's development and progress.

Open 9am-6pm April-September, 9am-5pm October-March. Closed Mondays. Admission is W1,500.

## Kongju Area

Kongju was one of the ancient capitals of the Paekche Kingdom and still retains many relics from that era.

*King Muryong's Tomb* was excavated in 1971. The burial chamber is lined with glazed tiles of a rough texture in a blend of bluish and brownish hues. The tomb is now sealed behind glass, but a detailed replica can be viewed at the museum.

*Kongju National Museum* was built to house the treasures of King Muryong's tomb. There are displays of striking golden jewellery and crowns which show the distinctive features of Paekche art.

## Puyo and Nonsan Area

Puyo was the last capital of the Paekche Kingdom and a place rich in legends. There are many remains, dating back to the kingdom's struggle against the Shilla Kingdom and its ally T'ang China in 660 AD. A steep hill in Puyo's city centre is the site of the Pusosansong Fortress where the Paekche forces made their last stand.

*Nak'waam Rock*, the 'Rock of Falling Flowers', is on top of the fortified hill. From here, a pavilion looks out on the Paengmagang River below. According to legend, 3000 ladies of the Paekche court leaped to their deaths into the river, committing mass suicide rather than yield to their conquerors.

The *Puyo National Museum* reopened in 1963. The new building has a display space of 2116m which is three times the size of the old one. It houses 7867 relics of the Paekche Kingdom including

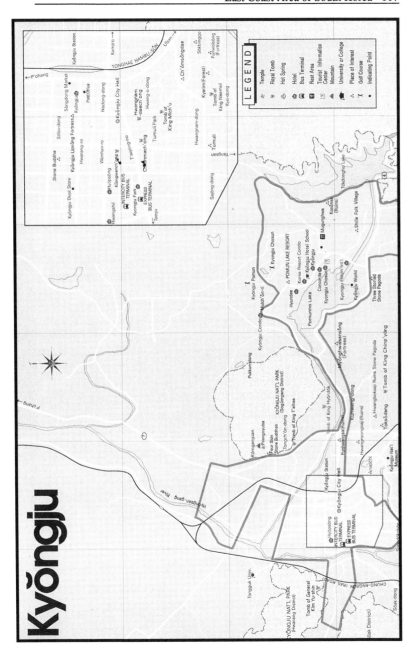

Gilt-bronze Seated Maitreya National Treasure no 83. Some of these show the cultural essence of the Paekche Kingdom and the cultural development of the Bronze Age in the Korean Peninsula. San 16-1, Tongnam-ri, Puyo'up, ph (0463) 33 8562/3. Closed Mondays.

*Taech'on Beach*, north-west of Puyo, is one of the oldest and most popular seaside resorts on the West Coast of Korea. It has broad sandy beaches and gentle tides making it ideal for swimming.

The *Unjin Miruk Buddha* is found at Kwanch'oksa Temple in Nonsan, a town just south-west of Puyo. This is Korea's largest stone statue of Buddha and it dates back to the 10th century. The appearance of the Buddha is rather odd. He has a small body, a large head and is wearing a lofty mortar-board-style hat.

# Chonju Area

Chonju is the capital of Chollabuk-do Province, and is famous for its many traditional houses. The 'Honam Rice Plain' lies to the west of Chonju. The city is the ancestral home of the royal branch of the Yi family, who ruled Korea during the Choson Dynasty, and there is a shrine honouring the ancestors of the clan. The city gate, a well-preserved example of Choson design and engineering, is one of the few to survive in the provincial areas.

*Kumsansa Temple*, 12.5km to the south-east of Chonju, is one of the largest and most important Buddhist shrines in the province. The original temple was built in 599AD and was enlarged in 1079.

*Mt Maisan* (Horse-Ears Mountain) is an hour's drive east of Chonju. It was given its name from the shape of its twin peaks when seen from certain angles. An easy climb leads to a curious site. A monk spent his life heaping up unmortared stones to form pagodas in a temple compound. Some of these pagodas are 10m (32 ft) high while others are just a few centimetres tall.

# Mt Naejangsan National Park

Mt Naejangsan is one of the five famous mountains of the Honam region, and the park is outstanding for its autumn colours.

The main peak is 722m (2,369 ft) high but there are many subsidiary peaks which can be reached by easy climbs. The mountain shares its name with Naejangsa Temple. There is also another temple, Paegyangsa, in the park.

# Kwangju Area

Kwangju is the capital of Chollanam-do Province, and the fourth largest city in the Republic of Korea. It has a population of 1.1 million and lies almost four hours directly south of Seoul by car or train. It is connected with Taegu to the east via the Olympic expressway.

*Kwangju National Museum* was built to house the precious Chinese porcelains that were salvaged in 1976 from a Chinese trading ship which was wrecked at Shinan 600 years before. San 83-3, Maegok-dong, Puk-gu, Kwangju, ph (062) 571 7111. Closed Mondays.

*Songgwangsa Temple*, south-east of Kwangju, is one of the largest temples in Korea. It was built as a shrine to the late Shilla Era but fell into disrepair until 1205 when it was reconstructed. Over the years this temple has produced a large number of famous monks.

# Mt Togyusan National Park

Muju and Kuch'ondong are two separate scenic areas within Mt Togyusan National Park. At the foot of the mountain, there are several first-class Korean inns. If you follow the mountain stream, you will come to Paengnyonsa Temple. A rainbow trout farm is also in this area.

# Mt Chirisan National Park

This mountain is famous for its beautiful scenery and superb hiking. With the expansion of the country's highways and transport network, it is relatively easy to reach from anywhere in the country. The autumn foliage is spectacular.
*Shilsangsa*, *Ssanggyesa* and *Hwaomsa Temples* are three important shrines in the area.

*Hwaomsa Temple*, located on the mountain's southern slopes near the town of Kurye, was founded in 544AD and is one of Korea's oldest temples. Its Kak'wangjon Hall, dating from the Chosan Period, is the largest existing wooden structure in Korea. A stone lantern nearby dates back to the ninth century. There are also other treasures, an excellent example being the stone pagoda supported by four lions from the Shilla Kingdom.

## Namwon

This country town is located at the north-western gateway to Mt Chirisan National park. Namwon is famous as the home of Ch'un-hyang, the legendary faithful maiden. A tourist complex with plenty of modern facilities is being developed here.

*Kwanghallu Pavilion* is in a park in Nawon. Ch'un-hyang and her true love are said to have first met here before circumstances threw them apart. There is a small shrine containing a portrait of this heroine who endured great hardships as she waited for her beloved's return. Each spring, a folk festival is held in Ch'un-hyang's honour.

If you wish to reach the southernmost tip, you can visit two islands, Chindo and Hongdo.
*Chindo Island* is a fascinating place to be in spring. The extreme tides make it possible to walk from the village of Hoedong to the small island of Modo. This is the Korean version of 'Moses Parting of the Red Sea Miracle'. It is celebrated with a variety of folk dances and performances, and attracts thousands of visitors in April and May.

*Hongdo Island* lies off the western tip of the Korean peninsula, and can be reached by ferry from Mokp'o. It is a favourite haunt for photographers because of its camellia forests and unusual rock formations. The island is isolated making it the perfect retreat for those who want to get away from it all.

# South-East Area

The south-east is a diverse and highly developed area, that is a blend of the ancient and modern. It is the home of the ancient Shilla Kingdom from which many relics remain. It also has several modern industrial cities.

After Seoul, Pusan is probably the Korean city that is best known to tourists. To the west of Pusan lies Kimhae International Airport which serves the needs of this vital area. A little further east is the industrial city of Masan and the industrial complex of Ch'angwon. To the south of Ch'angwon is the beautiful natural harbour of Chinhae, the home of the Republic of Korea's navy.

This south-eastern area is bounded on the west by the mighty Naktonggang River, which ends in an estuary west of Pusan. The estuary is the natural habitat of large numbers of migratory waterfowl. There is a fine network of roads in the south-east, including the Seoul-Pusan expressway and a highway linking Masan and Taegu. There are also good road connections linking Taegu with Ulsan and P'ohang to the east of Kyongu.

## Taegu Area

Taegu is Korea's third largest city after Seoul and Pusan. It is situated on both the railway and the expressway that links Seoul with Pusan and is the gateway to the Kyongju district to the east.

*Tonghwasa Temple* is only 22km from Taegu and can easily be reached by road. The temple was originally constructed in the Shilla period but was reconstructed in the Choson period. To the right of the entrance, overlooking the road, is an image of Buddha carved into the cliff face.

*Haeinsa Temple* is a two-hour drive south-west of Taegu. It is one of the jewels of Mt Kayasan National Park. It was established in 802AD and it safeguards a number of important historic and artistic treasures. It is chiefly known as the repository of the Tripitaka Koreana, a set of 80,000 wooden printing blocks engraved with one of the most comprehensive compilations of the Buddhist scriptures in all Asia. It took years to make the plates and although they were completed in 1252, they are in perfect condition and can still be used to print.

*Kyongju*, now a country town, was once one of the greatest cities in the world. It was the capital of the Shilla Kingdom and subsequently the whole of Korea when Shilla united the three ancient kingdoms in the late seventh century. Kyong is a fascinating place to visit.

Originally called Sorabol, it contains so many Shilla relics that it rightly deserves its name 'Museum of the World'.

A walking tour of Kyongju is best started from City Hall. All the sights are fairly close together.

*Tumuli Park* near Ch'omsongdae Observatory, holds 20 of the larger royal tombs, including the Ch'onmach'ong Tomb, which are found in great numbers in the area. There are 200 tombs, large and small, in the city and its environs and a hundred more scattered over the nearby countryside.

*Ch'omsongdae Observatory* is a seventh century bottle-shaped stone tower. Recent research has revealed that the tower was built according to complex mathematical principles. The 12 stones at the base seem to represent the months of the year and the 30 layers of stone are thought to symbolise the days of the month. The 24 stones which protrude from the tower at regular intervals show the seasonal subdivisions of the lunar calendar. There are 366 stones in all, representing the days of the year.

*Anapchi Pond* was a place where the Shilla royal family relaxed and enjoyed themselves. It lies just across the road from the former site of Panwolsong Fortress. The pond was temporarily drained in 1974 to reveal a treasure trove of Shilla artefacts. They found Buddhist statues, jewellery and even a fully outfitted royal barge perfectly preserved in its watery grave. These items are now on show in the Kyongju National Museum.

*Sokpinggo* is a well-preserved stone ice house in the grounds of the Panwolsong Fortress. More than 1000 stones were used to construct the 19m long, 6m wide and 5.4m high building.

*Punhwangsa Temple* no longer exists but its stone brick pagoda is still standing. The pagoda was originally nine stones high but now it only has three. Each of the four sides of the lowest story has a carved niche with a stone door half open and flanked by the guardian Deva kings.

*Kyerim Forest* is the birthplace of Korea's largest family, the Kims. According to legend, King T'alhae heard a cock crowing in the forest and upon investigation discovered a golden box hanging from a tree. He opened the box to find a lovely baby boy inside. He adopted the baby and named him Kim, which means 'gold'.

*Ch'onmach'ong*, or 'Heavenly Horse Tomb' is one of the excavated tombs in Tumuli Park. This tomb was discovered in 1973 and found to contain numerous gems and jewellery, ceramics, swords, horse trappings, crowns made of pure gold and a painting of a heavenly flying horse. The interior has been rebuilt to allow visitors to go inside and see how the tomb was constructed.

*Orung* (Five Tombs) is said to be the final resting place of the first Shilla king, Pak Hyokkose, his queen and three later kings. Nearby Najong Shrine is the legendary site where Pak Hyokkose was born.

*General Kim Yu-Shin's Tomb* is especially impressive. It is surrounded by well-preserved statues of humans and animals. There is also a fine set of Chinese zodiac animals carved in relief on stone slabs encircling the mound. General Kim Yu-Shin was the seventh century military leader whose armies united Korea.

*King Muyol's Tomb*, near General Kim Yu-Shin's tomb, is dated from the same period. It is distinguished by a stone monument in the style that was introduced during the United Shilla Period. It has a huge tortoise base with columns and an inscribed capstone.

*Pomun Lake Resort* is one of the most popular places in the Kyongju area, only fifteen minutes outside the city. The resort boasts the most modern and extensive facilities in Kyongju, and consists of four super-deluxe hotels, a convention centre, a championship golf course, a marina and a shopping centre. In addition, there are swimming pools, tennis courts, bowling alleys, a casino and pleasure boats. The resort is supplemented by a modern hotel school. Shuttle buses and a taxi service link the Pomun Lake Resort with downtown Kyongju and the historic sites in the area.

Guided tours are available on a regular or chartered basis. By staying at the resort, visitors experience the perfect combination of comfort, recreation and historic sights.

The *Kyongju National Museum*, 76, Inwang-dong, Kyongju, ph (056) 25 192, is on the outskirts of the city in a long, low building with upswept roof eaves in the traditional Korean style. The museum is a treasure house of objects excavated from Shilla tombs, including gold crowns, jewellery, ceramics, sword hilts and a lot of other fascinating relics. In the grounds of the museum stands the great bronze King Songdok's Bell, also called Emille Bell, which was cast in 771AD. It is one of the largest and most resonant bells in Asia. According to a tragic legend, a child was thrown into the molten metal when the bell was cast. Monks of the time attributed the unique tone of the bell to the child crying for its mother. 'Emi...emi...lie'! Closed Mondays.

A *Buddhist Triad*, made of stone, stands on the slope of Mt Namsan. The central figure is the Anita Buddha, or the Buddha of the Western Paradise, who welcomes believers if they recite his name with intense feeling. This image is 3m (10 ft) high and is characterised by a round, plump face and distinctive smile. He is flanked by two slightly smaller Bodhisattvas, which are Buddhas who have gained enlightenment.

*Sokkuram Grotto* was built on Mt To'hamsan above Pulguksa

Temple at about the same date. The grotto is accessible via a winding road through a scenic forest. It can also be reached on foot along a hiking path. Its great granite Buddha and the masterly bas-reliefs of guardian figures have been proclaimed as a pinnacle of East Asian Buddhist art. Its domed roof is also a feat of engineering that has stood the test of time.

A glass panel protects the grotto from humidity. The visitor can still go into the entrance and contemplate the exalted features of the huge Buddha who gazes towards the sea in the distant horizon.

*Mt Namsan* is truly a treasure trove of cultural remains. The average tourist could not possibly see everything but must see the stone relief carvings at Ch'il-buram (Seven Buddha Hermitage), which will prove to be an unforgettable experience and well worth the climb. These priceless objects of religious art are only surpassed by the Buddhist scriptures found in Sokkuram Grotto. There are many other interesting remains scattered throughout Mt Namsan and its valleys, that show this region's unique cultural heritage.

*P'osokchong Watercourse* is all that remains of a detached royal palace. It is an ancient miniature watercourse made of stone and looped round in the shape of an abalone shell from which it gets its name. The king used to hold drinking parties here, floating the cups round the loop to his guests.

*Pulguksa Temple* is Korea's best known temple. It is a monument to the skill of Korean architects and the depth of Buddhist faith at the time. Most of the wooden buildings have had to be rebuilt over the centuries, but the stone bridges, stairways and two famous pagodas, Tabot'ap and Sokkat'ap, are the originals. The temple, first built in 535AD was enlarged in 751AD. Today, the temple's form is as beautiful and charming as ever.

*Kwaerung* is a tomb near Pulguksa Temple. Legend has it that this is the grave of the 38th Shilla ruler, King Wonsong, who reigned at the end of the eighth century. Statues line the path leading up to the tomb symbolising civil and military officials in attendance on their ruler.

# Pusan

Pusan is Korea's principal port and second largest city. It is situated in a rounded depression between the surrounding mountains, a 'cauldron' from which the city derives its name. Being on the southern tip of the Korean Peninsula, it enjoys a milder climate than the rest of the country. The city is a true cosmopolitan port.

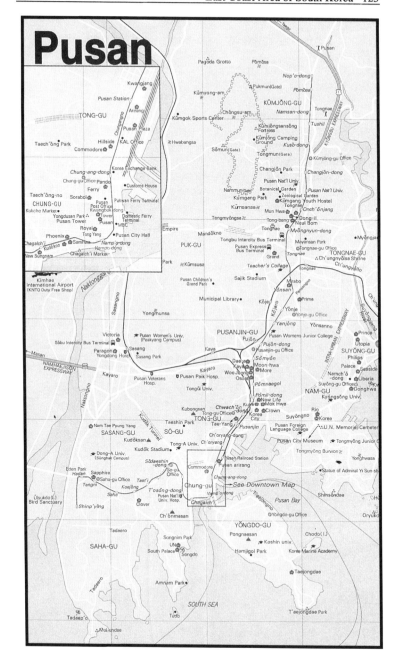

# Pusan

Ferries link it with Cheju-do Island and the Hallyosudo Waterway. They also ply the water between Pusan and Shimonoseki, Osaka, Kobe and Hakata in Japan. Pusan is a port of call for many international cruise and cargo ships, and has an international airport, Kimhae.

It is an expanding, modern city with broad streets and an up-to-date underground (subway) system. The underground connects downtown, Kwangbok-dong and Namp'o-dong with the suburbs. There are several ocean beach resorts, hot springs and Buddhist temples.

Once again, a walking tour is best started from City Hall.

The *Chagalch'i Fish Market* can be found on the dock-side. It is bustling with activity early in the morning when the fishermen bring in their catch. For those who have self-catering accommodation, it is the place to buy your fresh fish at a reasonable price. It is certainly a colourful scene for photographers.

*Yongdusan Park* provides a pleasant piece of greenery on a hilltop in the heart of the city of Pusan. It has an observation deck which gives the visitor a spectacular view of the city. There are several war memorials and a statue of Korea's great naval hero of the 16th century, Admiral Yi Sun-shin.

*Kumgang Park* is north-east of the downtown area, not far from the Tong-nae Hot Spring. It is natural and scenic with wooded slopes, sparkling streams and unusual rock formations. There are also carnival rides and other amusements for the young at heart.

*Tongnae Hot Spring* is an old medicinal town 14km north of the centre of Pusan. There are plenty of small hotels and inns which provide bathing facilities.

The *UN Memorial Cemetery* is a reminder of the Korean War (1950-53). It is up in the hills and is the resting place of many foreign soldiers who gave their lives in the conflict.

The *Municipal Museum of Pusan* is near the UN Memorial Cemetery. It has about 2000 priceless cultural artefacts.

*Pomosa Temple* is in the northern part of Pusan. It is one of the largest in Korea and was founded in 678AD. To approach the temple, you cross a gracefully arched stone bridge over a babbling brook then enter through artistic gates which guard the complex.

*T'Ongdosa Temple,* the 'Temple of Universal Salvation', is half-way between Pusan and Kyongju with its own exit off the Seoul-Pusan expressway. This road passes along the banks of a mountain stream through a grove of picturesque pines. There are several stone lanterns along the roadside, marking the way to the temple. The temple was founded in 646AD and is the home of some precious Buddhist relics.

*Haeundae Beach* is the most popular beach in Pusan. It can be reached by bus or local train in half-an-hour from downtown. Haeundae has a long, curving, sandy beach which is bounded on the west by Tongbaeksom Island. Although this rocky, wooded islet appears to be an island, it is joined to the mainland by a small isthmus. You will find hotels, including three of deluxe standard, inns and restaurants of various types and prices.

# Hallyosudo Waterway

The Hallyo Haesang National Park, better known as the Hallyosudo Waterway, stretches from Hansando Island in the east, past Ch'ungmu, Samch'onp'o and Namhaedo Island on to Odongdo Island and the industrial port of Yosu in the west. It is a marine park dotted with some 400 islands and islets, many uninhabited, with fantastic scenery. Hydrofoils operate a regular service between the two port cities of Pusan and Yosu.

*Kojedo Island*, just to the west of Hallyosudo Waterway, is the second largest of Korea's 3300 islands. It is noted for its beautiful pine trees, camellias, and its sheer cliffs that are the home of numerous sea birds. Small rocky reefs add to its beauty. The island has a number of monuments to Admiral Yi Sun-shin. There is a good beach at Kujora.

*Hansando Island* is of great historical importance. It was the site of fierce battles during the Japanese invasion in the late 16th century. Admiral Yi Sun-shin, the great hero, scored his first victory against the Japanese fleet off the waters of the island. His iron-clad ships were the key to the success. A turtle-shaped lighthouse commemorates his victory.

*Haegumgang* is an outcrop of rocks of spectacular beauty lying south of Kojedo Island.

*Namhaedo Island* is connected to the mainland by the Great Namhaedaegyo Bridge. This is the longest suspension bridge in the Orient. Namhaedo Island is made up of a series of peaks linked by valleys. The road runs down from the bridge through the city of Naamhae to the lovely Sangju Beach farther south.

*Samch'onp'o* is a sanctuary for the white heron, a protected species. *Odongdo Island* lies at the western end of the Hallyosudo Waterway. Its name means 'Paulownia Tree Island' but oddly enough, this tree does not grow on the island. Instead, a special type of bamboo grows here.

# Cheju-Do Island

Cheju-do Island is known as 'Korea's Honeymoon Capital'. It is the largest and the most famous of the 3300 islands. It covers an area of 1825 sq km and lies 96km off the tip of the Korean Peninsula. Being so far from the mainland, the Island has developed a unique culture. Cheju-do is only a one hour fight from Seoul and less from Pusan. There are direct flights from Tokyo, Osaka, Fukuoka, Sendai and Nagoya in Japan. It can also be reached by ferry from Pusan, Mokp'o and Wando Island.

Cheju-do is thriving on tourism. Other sources of income are tangerines, fishing, cattle and other agricultural products. The sub-tropical climate favours the agricultural industry.

The now extinct *Mt Hallasan* volcano has created a land of striking contrasts. The fields and forests are dark green, the oil seed rape flower bright yellow and the volcanic formations of basalt rock are a reddish-brown.

Tolharubang (basalt figures) are an ever-present sight on Cheju-do adding to its unique atmosphere. Some are fully life size 'stone grandfathers' while others are small enough to be souvenirs. Now treated as whimsical mascots, these figures are believed to have been venerated as village guardian deities in the past.

Green volcanic cones, a sub-tropical climate and clear waters have all contributed to making Cheju-do the first choice of Korean tourists and a place of charm and delight for overseas visitors.

*Cheju City* is centrally located on the north shore and is a thriving, modern tourist city.

The *Cheju-do Folklore and Natural History Museum* features a collection of folk crafts, tools and equipment as well as plants and minerals. It is extremely interesting and one of the best of its kind. 996-1, 11do 2-dong, Cheju, ph (064) 22 2465. Closed New Years Day and Ch'usok.

The *Cheju Folklore Museum* is ten minutes east of the city. It is a private museum and noted for its displays of clothing and tools used by the islanders in the past. 3-2505 Samyang-dong, Cheju, ph (064) 55 1976. Open daily.

# Chejudo

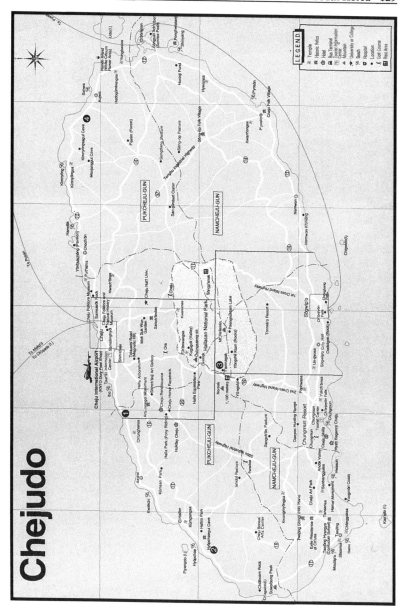

LEGEND
- Temple
- Historic Relics
- Hotel
- Bus Terminal
- Tourist Information
- University or College
- Mountain
- Beach
- Hospital
- Location
- Golf Course
- Rest Area

*Kwandokchong Pavilion* was built in 1448 and used for military training. The wooden, painted beams are typical of the Choson Period.

*Samsonghyol Holes* are found near the Paradise Cheju Hotel in the city. According to legend, three demons named Ko, Pu and Yang came out of the three holes in the meadow and founded the island's first families. Every April, October and December, the descendants of the three clans gather together to honour their forefathers.

*Mok Suk Won Park* is a public park. It contains a variety of unusual rocks and storm-polished pieces of wood collected from around the island. It is at the entrance of Cheju National University, a few minutes south of Cheju City on the First Cross-Island Highway.

*Yongduam* (Dragon Rock) is an unusual lava formation on the coast west of Cheju City. It gets its name from the basalt head which appears to be a dragon with an open mouth about to roar. It is a popular site.

### East Coast Area
*Songsan Ilch'ulbong* (Sunrise Peak) on the eastern tip of Cheju-do Island is one of the many cones that dot the land. There is a trail which leads up the western edge of the crater, rising sharply up the side of the cone. It is a narrow, steep path but from the top there is a fantastic view. It is at its best at sunrise.

*Songsanp'o* literally means 'Fortress Mountain Port'. It is a small fishing village which takes its name from the Songsan Peak.

*Udo (Cow) Island* can be reached by regular ferry service from Songsanp'o. It is worth a visit but you must allow most of a full day.

### North Shore
The north shore is famous for the fine beaches of Hamdok, Iho and Hyopchae, all easily accessible from the city. Each has accommodation and restaurants.

*Kimnyongsagul Cave* or 'Snake Cave' is near the village of Kimnyong. The local legend tells of a huge demon serpent living in the lava tube. To prevent any misfortunes, the locals had to sacrifice a beautiful virgin to the serpent.

They continued to do this every year until their brave governor killed the beast.

*Manjanggul Cave* is also near Kimnyong village. It is the longest lava tube in the world at 13.4km.

### South Coast Area

*Sogwip'o City* is the major city of the south coast, and is connected to Cheju city by the First and Second Cross-Island Highways. It has a mild sub-tropical climate all year and produces quantities of tangerines and pineapples. There is fantastic scenery in the area along with waterfalls, forests and a rugged coastline.

*Chongbang Waterfall* lies to the east of the city. This spectacular cascade plunges straight into the sea.

*Ch'onjiyon Waterfall*, to the west of Sogwip'o city, falls into a gorge surrounded by lush sub-tropical vegetation. It is well worth a visit.

### West Coast Area

*Hallim* is the major centre on the west coast. It is a thriving fishing port. The Hallim Weavers make visitors welcome, and you can see the whole process of weaving from the wool as it is collected from the sheep to the final product. There are exquisite shawls, scarfs, gloves, cloth, blankets and many more items available in the attached shop.

*Hyopchaegul Cave* is a well-known tourist attraction on the southern outskirts of Hallim. Winds have blown calcium-rich sand over the ground and the rain has washed the calcium down into the cave, where it has formed icicle-like stalagmites and stalactites.

*Ishidol Ranch*, in the hills behind Hallim, is a cattle and sheep property. It is a co-operative venture begun by the Catholic Church.

*Cholbuam Rock* is a 20-minute drive south of Hallim. It is a beautiful and intriguing rock formation which lies just off the shore, and is said to be a fisherman's wife waiting for her husband to return from sea.

*Sanbanggulsa Grotto* is on a hill in the south-western corner of Cheju-do island. It now contains a seated image of Buddha, but was once occupied by a hermit monk. The view from the front of the grotto makes it well worth the climb.

## Activities

Blessed with a rugged landscape from rocky mountains to sparkling seas, Cheju-do Island has something for everyone.

**Boating** can be enjoyed aboard the glass bottom boats, *Elizabeth* and *Yonggung* which enable passengers to view life in the sea. The one-hour cruise, near the eastern fishing town of Songsanp'o, costs W5,000.

**Casinos** can be found in the Cheju KAL Hotel, the Hyatt Regency, the Cheju Shilla, Cheju Grand, the Oriental, the Cheju Nam Seoul and Seogwipo KAL.

**Fishing** is a year-round shore and deep-sea sport. Current information regarding season, location and tackle can be obtained from travel agents or your hotel staff.

**Golf** can be played on Cheju-do's three courses - Chungmun, Oraand and Cheju.

**Hunting** can be indulged on Cheju-do Island. Duck and pheasant are the most popular game birds. (*see Sport*)

**Mountain Climbing** enthusiasts can climb the island's voclanoe amd its many subsidiary peaks.

**Scuba Diving** is ideal in the clear waters and very popular with a growing number of Korean and overseas scuba diving enthusiasts. All the equipment can be rented from the scuba diving centre.

**Submarine Trips** are the ideal way to see the underwater world. A half-hour trip with the *Daekuk Subsea Co Ltd* costs W49,500. Their submarine is equipped with observation windows on either side and at the rear. For bookings phone (02) 774-9981 or (064) 32-6060.

**Swimming** is possible on the beaches along Cheju-do's coastline.

**Women Divers**, *haenyo*, are the most famous attraction of Cheju-do Island. These women dive to incredible depths to harvest seaweed and shellfish.

# Tours

There is no shortage of conducted tours in any part of South Korea, and travel agents abound. Some specialise in local tours of Seoul and major cities, others do long distance excursions lasting several days. Sightseeing tours can be arranged for groups on request. The cost is based on a party of ten.

Special interest tours can also be organised. These range from two days of nothing but shopping in Seoul at a cost of US$240, to an in-depth twelve day tour of South Korea for US$1530.

If you have not pre-booked your sightseeing, all tourist hotels have brochures and can make a booking for you. If you wish to make a reservation yourself and can't decide which agent to approach, the Korea Travel Bureau, which is government run, is the best place to contact. They can be found at 1465-11 Soch'o 3 dong, Soch'o-gu, Seoul, ph (02) 585-1191, fax (02) 585-1187. They also have an office in the Hotel Lotte. All regular tours take the same routes and are about the same price. To save congestion, they do not all visit the same attraction at the same time. One company may visit a palace in the morning and another have the same palace on their afternoon itinerary.

## Tour to Panmunjom

It is the most popular tour and can only be taken with the Korea Travel Bureau. For centuries Panmunjom was a place no one cared about except the few people who lived there. It has always been a farm village. But, now it stands right in the middle of the *Demilitarised Zone* that lies between North and South Korea. This zone is 243km long and stretches from the Han River in the west to just below the 39th parallel on the east coast of the peninsula. There is a 4000m strip down the centre, and it was here, in the obscure village of Panmunjom, that an Armistice was signed, ending the three year Korean War. It has been the pivot for on-going talks, a point for north-south contacts and the guardian of the longest truce in modern times. It takes a visit to this hamlet to understand a country divided with a people longing for re-unification.

The tour runs weekdays unless military or other official business prevents entry to the Joint Security Area. It is essential to pre-book and to check the day before departure for the time the bus will leave the Hotel Lotte. There are no pick-ups at other hotels. You must be at the Korea Travel Bureau's Office, in the Hotel Lotte, 20 minutes before departure time. The tour takes about seven hours and costs W45,000, lunch included. Passports must be carried, and children under 10 are not allowed to join the tour.

Jeans, shorts and sandals are not permitted. Shaggy or unkempt hair is not allowed. Any equipment, microphones or flags belonging to the Communist side in the conference room must not be touched. You must on no account speak, make any gesture toward or in any way approach or respond to personnel from the other side.

The buses from Seoul travel along the T'ongillo (Unification) Highway then across Freedom Bridge to reach the truce camp. Two stops are made on the way to look at statues of the heroes of the Korean War and for restrooms.

You will be given a briefing before lunch which is served in the UN mess. Time will be allowed for purchases to be made from the Duty Free shop. After this you will board your bus once more.

Your military guide will instruct you on what you may take with you when you leave the bus at the joint security camp. Cameras are allowed but nothing else. It is advisable to wear something which has pockets so you can put your money in them. You will be taken to Freedom House, a pagoda type construction that offers a great view of North Korea. Next, you walk a few metres and cross the demarcation line to the conference huts. Your guide will give a talk while two armed North Korean guards stand close by at the head of the table, and others peer through the windows.

The tour buses stop twice after you leave the demarcation camp so that tourists can have a view of the area. The Bridge of No Return is where the South Koreans have a check point looking at the check point belonging to the North Koreans. No stops are made on the way back to Seoul.

## Morning Tour of Seoul

Kyongbokkung Palace (T'oksugung Palace on Tuesdays), National Museum (Folklore Museum on Tuesdays), Chogyesa Temple,

It'aewon shopping street. Daily. Cost W19,000. Time 9am-noon, KTB 10am-1pm.

# Afternoon Tour of Seoul

Ch'angdokkung Palace, Secret Garden (Ch'anggyonggung Palace on Monday), Chogyesa Temple, East Gate Market. Daily. Cost W19,000. Time 2-5pm.

# Full Day Tour

Kyongbokkung Palace, National Folklore Museum, Chogyesa Temple, Ginseng Shop/Amethyst Factory, Mt Namsan Tower, Olympic Stadium, Han-gang River Cruise. Some tours include Lotte World Adventure which is a better tour for those with children.

Daily. Cost W58,000 including lunch. Time 9am-5.30pm.

# Night Tours

*Shereton Walker Hill.* This hotel has its own theatre where traditional music and dance are performed as well as western shows from Europe. You will have dinner, see the show and have time to visit the casino. Daily 6-10pm. Cost W78,000.

*Korea House Dinner and Show.* On this tour, you drive to the restaurant on Mt Namsan for an excellent Korean dinner, followed by traditional music and dance. Daily. Cost W66,000. Time 6-10pm.

# Tours in Seoul Vicinity

Olympic Stadium, Korean Folk Village (lunch), Lotte World Adventure, It'aewon shopping street. Daily. Cost W58,000 includes tickets to Lotte World. Time 10am-6pm.

Seoul-Korean Folk Village-Seoul costs W30,000 including lunch. Time 1-5pm.

# Tours outside Seoul

### Two Day Tours

*Seoul-Mt Soraksan* for a full day tour. Overnight at a good hotel. Return to Seoul following day. Cost W160,000. Departure time 8am.

*Seoul-Kyongju* for full day tour. Overnight at a good hotel. Return to Seoul following day. Cost W200,000. Departure time 8am.

### Three Day Tours

*Seoul-Kyongju* for full day tour. Overnight at an hotel. Travel on to Pusan for a full day tour. Overnight Pusan. Return to Seoul. Tours return by Express train. Cost W300,000. Departure time 8am.

*Seoul-Cheju-do* for two full day island tours. Accommodation in first class hotel twin share with American breakfast. Single supplement W30,000 per night. Tours conducted by English speaking guide. Japanese and Chinese guides on request. Minimum booking two persons. Cost W456,000. Departure time 8am.

Longer tours can be arranged. It is advisable to make reservations for these through your travel agent in your home country. Prices for tours of more than three days are quoted in US dollars. For more information about the attractions, refer to *Sightseeing*.

# Tours of North Korea

Tours to what is known as 'The Hermit Kingdom' are organised by the North Korean government and the itinerary can be changed without notice. The standard 15 day tour can either be taken from Bangkok where a visa can be issued, flying direct to P'yongyang, the capital of North Korea, or from Beijing. On the latter there is a tour of Beijing before the flight to P'yongyang. Visas for North Korea payable in China cost US$15.

Accommodation for six or more people in a group will be in first class hotels. For two to five people, the price is unchanged but accommodation will be in tourist class hotels. The rates include all meals, beer and soft drinks.

The itinerary begins in P'yongyang, the capital, on the banks of the Poyong and Taedong Rivers, and the day is at leisure. It is a modern city with wide, leafy streets abounding with immense 'Socialist' monuments. There is Kim Il Sung square, the 46m (150 ft) high statue of the horse Chollima and the 170m (560 ft) tower of the Juche Idea. The Underground Railway is decorated with murals similar to the one in Moscow.

The following day, you travel to Kaesong, the ancient capital of the Koryo Dynasty 918-1392. It is a charming, picturesque city full of historical relics, and is well known for ginseng and celadon ware. From here, a tour is taken to the Demilitarised Zone at Panmunjom. After which, you return to P'yongyang city where a visit is made to the Children's Palace, a massive structure of 500 rooms, where school children develop special talents.

The next day, there is a coach trip to Mt Kumgang via the port of Wonsan, noted for its beaches. Mt Kumgang is an eerie, beautiful creation of nature, consisting of thick forests, waterfalls and raging torrents set amidst 12,000 craggy pinnacles. A visit is also made to tranquil Kuryong pool and Samil lagoon. This area is known as one of the eight wonders of the Orient. The coach returns to P'yongyang for the night.

Day four offers a change of pace with a train ride through beautiful countryside to Mt Myohyang, and a visit to the vast International Friendship Exhibition built into the mountain. On display, are thousands of lavish gifts from over 150 countries. A visit is also made to Pohyon Temple built in 1042.

The tour passes through spectacular scenery, with many waterfalls, pools, pavilions and Buddhist hermitages as it heads for Sangwon valley on the way back to P'yongyang. There is a visit to the Grand Peoples study house, which is ten stories high, has 750,000 blue tiles, 34 roofs and much more. The tour ends after lunch. Tour costs vary depending on where the journey begins, but to give some idea, from Australia the price is around US$4000.

# Travel Agents

### Seoul

*Central Express Tours*, 115 Toryom-dong, Chumg-gu, ph (02) 725 0891/5, fax (02)725 0890.

*Global Sightseeing*, Sam Jin Building 148-4, Ulchiro 2-ga, Chung-gu, ph (02) 278 0616/9, fax (02) 278 0135.

Reliance Travel, 3 fl, Eemo Building, Samsong-dong, Kangnam-gu, ph (02) 547 8855, fax (02) 543 1689.

*Yusei Travel*, 18-2 Tohwa-dong, Map'o-gu, ph (02) 718 4728, fax (02) 718 4726.

### Pusan

Choson Travel, 658 Chonp'o 4-dong, Chin-gu, ph (051) 816 8661, fax (051) 816 8574.

Hanmaeum Family Tours, 1-61 Sujong-dong, Tong-gu, ph (051) 644 8003, fax (051) 241 2171.

*Woo Joo Travel Service*, 53-17 Chungang-dong, 4-ga, Chung-gu, ph (051) 462 2215/7, fax (051) 463 2218.

### Inch'on
*New Hareubang Tourist*, 206-3 Chuan-dong, Nam-gu, ph (032) 872 6006, fax (032) 872 6005.

### Taegu
*Surabul Travel*, 20 Tongin-dong, Chung-gu, ph (053) 423 0011, fax (053) 423 0018.

### Kwang-ju
*Nakla Tours*, 81-2 Kumnamno 4-ga, Tong-gu, ph (062) 222 5900, fax (062) 232 3590.

### Ch'ungch'ongbuk-do
*Daeil Tour Kaebal*, 162-7 Pungmunno 2-ga, Ch'ongju, ph (043) 57 0100, fax (043) 57 0102.

### Chollabuk-do
*Daehan Air Travel Service*, 602-24, Sonosong-dong, Tokjin-gu, Chongju, ph (0652) 85 7758, fax (0652) 85 3311.

### Kyongsangnam-do
*Saewon Air Travel Service*, 321 Saho-dong, Masan, ph (0551) 46 7161/3, fax (0551) 44 4997.

### Cheju-do
*Cheju Tourist Service Co*, 300-1 Yon-daong, Cheju, ph (064) 46 6111, fax (064) 42 7800.
*Korea Tours*, 321-13 LLdo 2-dong, Cheju, ph (064) 58 2051/4, fax (064) 58 2055.
*Yoona Travel Service*, 533 Samdo 1-dong, Cheju, ph (064) 56 5711, fax (064) 56 5715.

# National Parks

Korea is a mountainous country, yet it has few peaks above 2000m. The mountain beauty is not intimidating but rather familiar and accessible. The harmony of the forested slopes, rocks, secluded Buddhist Temples and mountain streams charm Korean and foreign visitors alike.

Scattered throughout Korea are 20 National Parks and many provincial parks which have been set aside so that everyone can enjoy the beauty of Korea's natural surroundings.

The entrance fee to these national parks is W600. It is sometimes higher in areas that include temples with national treasures.

### Mt Puk'ansan National Park
Located 30 minutes drive to the north of downtown Seoul, Mt Puk'ansan (836m) provides good hiking and rock climbing. Area - 157 sq km.

### Mt Odaesan National Park
Located to the south of Mt Soraksan, Mt Odaesan (1563m) is the home of Wolchongsa Temple with its octagonal pagoda and Sanwonsa Temple. Area - 298 sq km.

### Mt Soraksan National Park
Located just outside the eastern port city of Sokch'o, Mt Sorakson (1708m) is one of the most beautiful mountains in Korea. It is famous for its granite peaks, lush green valleys, mysterious temples and glorious waterfalls. Area - 373 sq km.

### Mt Ch'iaksan National Park
Located about 11km east of Wonju in Kangwon-do Province, Mt Ch'iaksan (1288m) is the site of Kuryongsa Temple which keeps alive many mountain legends. Area - 182 sq km.

## Mt Sobaeksan National Park
Mt Sobaeksan (1439m) soars at the outset of Sobaeksanmaek Mountain Range. Its Pusoksa Temple is noted for some of the oldest wooden architecture in Korea. Area - 320 sq km.

## Mt Woraksan National Park
Situated three hours south-east of Seoul, Mt Woraksan (1162m) is close to the well-known Suanbo Hot Springs, Ch'ungju Dam Reservoir and Tayang P'algyong (Eight Scenic Wonders of the Tanyang area). Area - 284 sq km.

## Mt Songnisan National Park
Located about 18km east of Poun, Ch'ungch'ongbuk Province, Mt Songnisan (1057m) is the home of the Popchusa Temple where Asia's tallest gilt bronze Buddha statue is found. Area - 283 sq km.

## Mt Kyeryongsan National Park
Located 30 minutes' drive west of Taejon, Mt Kyeryongsan (845m) has many beautiful temples including Tonghaksa (famous for its cherry blossoms in spring) and Kapsa. Area - 61 sq km.

## Mt Togyusan National Park
Located 90 minutes' drive south-east of Taejon, Mt Togyusan (1594m) is famous for its beautiful scenery. Area - 219 sq km.

## Mt Kayasan National Park
Located 30 minutes' drive west of Taejon, Mt Kayasan (1430m) National Park is the site of Korea's best-known temple, Haeinsa. This temple houses the 80,000 wooden printing blocks of the Tripitaka Koreana, the most complete collection of Buddhist scriptures in Asia. Area - 79 sq km.

## Mt Chirisan National Park
Located about 137km north-east of Kwangju, Mt Chirisan (1915m) was the first National Park designated in Korea. It is best known for the Hwaomsa Temple which contains many national treasures. Area - 440 sq km.

## Mt Naejangsan National Park

Located between Chonju and Kwangju, Mt Naejangsan (763m) boasts glorious autumn foliage and the Paegyangsa Temple. Area - 76 sq km.

## Pyonsanbando National Park

Located on a peninsula in south-western Chollabuk-do, the park is famous for splendid old temples scattered throughout its scenic mountains. Area - 157 sq km.

## Mt Wolch'ulsan National Park

Located about 26km west of Mokp'o, Chollanam-do Province, Mt Wolch'ulsan (809m) stands in the middle of the Honam Plain and has splendid rock formations, beautiful camellias and exotic temples. Area - 41 sq km.

## Mt Hallasan National Park

Mt Hallasan (1950m) on Chejudo Island, is the highest mountain in the Republic of Korea. It is an extinct volcano and is particularly famous for its flora and fauna. Area - 149 sq km.

## Tadohae Haesang National Park

Located on the south-western tip of the Korean Peninsula, this maritime park is comprised of many beaches and islands. Hongdo Island is famous for its camellia forests and unusual rock formations. Area - 2344 sq km.

## Hallyo Haesang National Park

This maritime park is a stretch of water 172km long. It runs from Hansando Island, south of Pusan, to Yosu in the west, and encompasses some 400 islands and islets. Area - 478 sq km.

# Captions to Photographs

| | |
|---|---|
| Facing inside front cover: | Ch'anggyonggung Palace grounds |
| Facing half title page: | Traditional Korean crafts |
| Facing page 16: | Traditional Korean bride |
| Facing page 17: | Korean Mask sculptor |
| Facing page 64: | Seoul's Naedaemun Gate at night |
| Facing page 65: | Samul-nori (Farmers Dance) |
| Facing page 80: | Autumn colours of Mt Soraksan Nat. Park |
| Facing page 81: | Detail of Sudoksa Temple |
| Inside backcover: | Pulguksa Temple |

# Index to Maps

# Index

## General

## Places & Attractions